Bootstrap for Rails

A quick-start guide to developing beautiful
web applications with the Bootstrap toolkit
and Rails framework

Syed Fazle Rahman

BIRMINGHAM - MUMBAI

Bootstrap for Rails

First published: February 2015

Production reference: 1190215

Published by Packt Publishing Ltd.

Livery Place

35 Livery Street

Birmingham B3 2PB, UK.

ISBN 978-1-78398-726-9

www.packtpub.com

Credits

Author
Syed Fazle Rahman

Reviewers
Fabrice Estiévenart

Samuel Goebert

Moncef Maiza

Commissioning Editor
Amarabha Banerjee

Acquisition Editor
Vinay Argekar

Content Development Editor
Ritika Singh

Technical Editor
Naveenkumar Jain

Copy Editor
Neha Vyas

Project Coordinator
Aboli Ambardekar

Proofreaders
Simran Bhogal

Linda Morris

Indexer
Rekha Nair

Production Coordinator
Komal Ramchandani

Cover Work
Komal Ramchandani

About the Author

Syed Fazle Rahman is an experienced frontend developer. He has published many frontend articles for SitePoint.com and HTMLxprs.com. His articles on Bootstrap framework are amongst the most popular ones in the web. He is enthusiastic about start-ups and likes technical writing/editing.

He is the cofounder of devmag.io — a network for developers and technologists. devmag.io helps technology enthusiasts connect and discover various programming and technology content.

About the Reviewers

Fabrice Estiévenart (@fab_estievenart) is a web and mobile developer with a focus on web frameworks (such as Yii, Django, AngularJS, NodeJS, and so on), big data technologies (such as Hadoop, MongoDB, Solr, and so on), and game libraries (such as LibGDX). He has initiated and contributed to many open source projects, such as Nutch (the highly extensible and scalable WebCrawler), GnuCash, Yii, and RetroWeb (a visual web wrapping application).

As a passionate video and board gamer, he has created LudoPassion (@ludopassion), where he offers to organize custom team building activities around serious games. In this context, he regularly publishes videos wherein he presents a few board games and explains their rules.

Finally, he is a solo guitarist/mandolinist (@fabrisss), trying to find some spare time to record his first full-length album with folk and bluegrass inspiration.

Samuel Goebert is a computer science PhD student at the Plymouth University, UK. Goebert has over 12 years of experience in software development and associated technologies. To know more about him, refer to https://www.linkedin.com/in/samuelgoebert.

www.PacktPub.com

Support files, eBooks, discount offers, and more

For support files and downloads related to your book, please visit www.PacktPub.com.

Did you know that Packt offers eBook versions of every book published, with PDF and ePub files available? You can upgrade to the eBook version at www.PacktPub.com and as a print book customer, you are entitled to a discount on the eBook copy. Get in touch with us at service@packtpub.com for more details.

At www.PacktPub.com, you can also read a collection of free technical articles, sign up for a range of free newsletters and receive exclusive discounts and offers on Packt books and eBooks.

https://www2.packtpub.com/books/subscription/packtlib

Do you need instant solutions to your IT questions? PacktLib is Packt's online digital book library. Here, you can search, access, and read Packt's entire library of books.

Why subscribe?

- Fully searchable across every book published by Packt
- Copy and paste, print, and bookmark content
- On demand and accessible via a web browser

Free access for Packt account holders

If you have an account with Packt at www.PacktPub.com, you can use this to access PacktLib today and view 9 entirely free books. Simply use your login credentials for immediate access.

Table of Contents

Preface

Howdy! So, you want to learn Bootstrap and its awesomeness and implement it in a Rails project? I think you made the right choice by selecting this book.

Web designing is not everyone's cup of tea. I have seen many experienced web developers who are extremely poor at web designing. They have the ability to make the most powerful applications, but lack the skills to create a decent looking website.

On the other hand, there's a sudden rise in the popularity of CSS and JavaScript frontend frameworks. These frameworks let the users create popular CSS and JavaScript components, such as drop-down menus, responsive menus, a proper grid system to structure websites, and so on easily without having any knowledge about CSS and JavaScript coding. Bootstrap, being one of the pioneers in the book, provides many prestyled CSS components that come ready to be used. You simply need to know the appropriate HTML files to use these frontend frameworks.

This book will help you understand what Bootstrap is, and how it can be used in a Rails environment. It will guide you through various CSS and JavaScript components of Bootstrap via many practical examples. If you are a Sass developer, this book will help you identify various Sass variables to customize Bootstrap.

I hope you have fun reading this book!

What this book covers

Chapter 1, *Introducing Web Application Development in Rails*, focuses on how to beautify Rails applications through the help of Bootstrap. This explanation is followed by the summary of this chapter.

Chapter 2, Introducing Bootstrap 3, will show you how to download and use Bootstrap in Rails projects.

Chapter 3, Powering a Rails App with Bootstrap's Grid System, will take you through Bootstrap's grid system and then proceed to show you how to use it in our first example application.

Chapter 4, Using Bootstrap's Typography, Buttons and Images in a Rails Application, focuses more on how to style a website's content such as text, links, and images.

Chapter 5, Reinventing Tables and Forms in Bootstrap, will take a look at the various features of Bootstrap tables and forms. In this chapter, we will first create dummy products and then integrate them in our real application.

Chapter 6, Creating Navigation Bars, will teach you how to create a Bootstrap navigation bar, and how we can modify it to fit our needs.

Chapter 7, Various Other Bootstrap Components, will explore some more Bootstrap components, which come ready to use.

Chapter 8, Working with Bootstrap Modals, will teach you how to create a Bootstrap modal and its various types and functionalities. We will also integrate a modal component in our Rails application.

Chapter 9, Creating Image Slideshows with Bootstrap Carousel, will get you started with the Bootstrap Carousel, how to add captions to the slides, and how to customize the Carousel.

Chapter 10, Creating a Shopping Cart Using Bootstrap Modals, is all about implementing what we have learned so far in Bootstrap. This chapter will definitely clear some of the core concepts of Bootstrap such as how to use Bootstrap modal, typography, buttons, and responsive tables.

Appendix, Adding Custom Styles to a Rails Application, talks about how to add a custom style to a Rails application, which is powered by a Bootstrap framework.

What you need for this book

You need the following to work with the examples in this book:

- Bootstrap version 3.3.1
- Rails version 4.2

Who this book is for

This book is for web developers who have a basic understanding of Ruby on Rails. You should definitely have prior knowledge of HTML and how it works. However, it is not necessary that you have prior knowledge of CSS and JavaScript for this book.

Conventions

In this book, you will find a number of styles of text that distinguish between different kinds of information. Here are some examples of these styles, and an explanation of their meaning.

Code words in text, database table names, folder names, filenames, file extensions, pathnames, dummy URLs, user input, and Twitter handles are shown as follows: "Let's create a folder named `Bootstrap_Rails_Project`."

A block of code is set as follows:

```
a{
display: block;
text-decoration: none;
width: 100px;
margin: 10px auto;
padding: 5px;
text-align: center;
background: #ccc;
color: #444;
font-size: 20px;
box-shadow: 4px 4px 0px #888;
font-weight: bold;
}
```

Any command-line input or output is written as follows:

```
rails new TODO
```

New terms and **important words** are shown in bold. Words that you see on the screen, in menus or dialog boxes for example, appear in the text like this: "Click on the **New Todo** now."

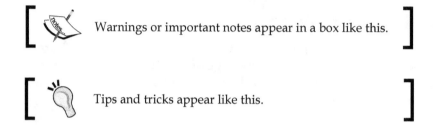

> Warnings or important notes appear in a box like this.

> Tips and tricks appear like this.

Reader feedback

Feedback from our readers is always welcome. Let us know what you think about this book—what you liked or may have disliked. Reader feedback is important for us to develop titles that you really get the most out of.

To send us general feedback, simply send an e-mail to feedback@packtpub.com, and mention the book title via the subject of your message.

If there is a topic that you have expertise in and you are interested in either writing or contributing to a book, see our author guide on www.packtpub.com/authors.

Customer support

Now that you are the proud owner of a Packt book, we have a number of things to help you to get the most from your purchase.

Downloading the example code

You can download the example code files for all Packt books you have purchased from your account at http://www.packtpub.com. If you purchased this book elsewhere, you can visit http://www.packtpub.com/support and register to have the files e-mailed directly to you.

Errata

Although we have taken every care to ensure the accuracy of our content, mistakes do happen. If you find a mistake in one of our books—maybe a mistake in the text or the code—we would be grateful if you would report this to us. By doing so, you can save other readers from frustration and help us improve subsequent versions of this book. If you find any errata, please report them by visiting http://www.packtpub.com/submit-errata, selecting your book, clicking on the **errata submission form** link, and entering the details of your errata. Once your errata are verified, your submission will be accepted and the errata will be uploaded on our website, or added to any list of existing errata, under the Errata section of that title. Any existing errata can be viewed by selecting your title from http://www.packtpub.com/support.

Piracy

Piracy of copyright material on the Internet is an ongoing problem across all media. At Packt, we take the protection of our copyright and licenses very seriously. If you come across any illegal copies of our works, in any form, on the Internet, please provide us with the location address or website name immediately so that we can pursue a remedy.

Please contact us at copyright@packtpub.com with a link to the suspected pirated material.

We appreciate your help in protecting our authors, and our ability to bring you valuable content.

Questions

You can contact us at questions@packtpub.com if you are having a problem with any aspect of the book, and we will do our best to address it.

1
Introducing Web Application Development in Rails

Presenting your application in the best possible way has been the most important factor for every web developer for ages. In this mobile-first generation, we are forced to go with the wind and make our application compatible with Mobiles, Tables, PCs, and every possible display on Earth.

Bootstrap is the one stop solution for all woes that developers have been facing. It creates beautiful responsive designs without any extra efforts and without any advanced CSS knowledge. It is a true boon for every developer.

In this chapter, and throughout the book, we will be focusing on how to beautify our Rails applications through the help of Bootstrap. In this chapter, we will create a basic Todo application with Rails. We will explore the folder structure of a Rails application and analyze which folders are important for templating a Rails Application. This will be helpful if you want to quickly revisit Rails concepts.

We will also see how to create views, link them, and also style them. The styling in this chapter will be done traditionally through the application's default CSS files. Finally, we will discuss how we can speed up the designing process using Bootstrap.

In short, we will cover the following topics:

- Why Bootstrap with Rails?
- Setting up a Todo Application in Rails
- Analyzing folder structure of a Rails application
- Creating views
- Styling views using CSS
- Challenges in traditionally styling a Rails Application

Why Bootstrap with Rails?

Rails is one the most popular Ruby frameworks which is currently at its peak, both in terms of demand and technology trend. With more than 3,100 members contributing to its development, and tens of thousands of applications already built using it, Rails has created a standard for every other framework in the Web today.

Rails was initially developed by David Heinemeier Hansson in 2003 to ease his own development process in Ruby. Later, he became generous enough to release Rails to the open source community. Today, it is popularly known as **Ruby on Rails**.

Rails shortens the development life cycle by moving the focus from reinventing the wheel to innovating new features. It is based on the convention of the configurations principle, which means that if you follow the Rails conventions, you would end up writing much less code than you would otherwise write.

Bootstrap, on the other hand, is one of the most popular frontend development frameworks. It was initially developed at Twitter for some of its internal projects. It makes the life of a novice web developer easier by providing most of the reusable components that are already built and are ready to use. Bootstrap can be easily integrated with a Rails development environment through various methods. We can directly use the .css files provided by the framework, or can extend it through its Sass version and let Rails compile it.

> Sass is a CSS preprocessor that brings logic and functionality into CSS. It includes features like variables, functions, mixins, and others. Using the Sass version of Bootstrap is a recommended method in Rails. It gives various options to customize Bootstrap's default styles easily.

Bootstrap also provides various JavaScript components that can be used by those who don't have any real JavaScript knowledge. These components are required in almost every modern website being built today.

Bootstrap with Rails is a deadly combination. You can build applications faster and invest more time to think about functionality, rather than rewrite codes.

Setting up a Todo application in Rails

Since this book is targeted for Rails developers, I assume that you already have basic knowledge of Rails development. You should also have Rails and Ruby installed in your machine to start with.

While writing this book, Ruby 2.1.1 and Rails 4.1.4 was used.

Let's first understand what this Todo application will do. Our application will allow us to create, update, and delete items from the Todo list. We will first analyze the folders that are created while scaffolding this application and which of them are necessary for templating the application.

So, let's dip our feet into the water:

1. First, we need to select our workspace, which can be any folder inside your system. Let's create a folder named `Bootstrap_Rails_Project`. Now, open the terminal and navigate to this folder.

2. It's time to create our Todo application. Write the following command to create a Rails application named TODO:

   `rails new TODO`

3. This command will execute a series of various other commands that are necessary to create a Rails application. So, just wait for sometime before it stops executing all the codes. If you are using a newer version of Rails, then this command will also execute `bundle install` command at the end. Bundle install command is used to install other dependencies.

The output for the preceding command is as follows:

```
      create  public/robots.txt
      create  test/fixtures
      create  test/fixtures/.keep
      create  test/controllers
      create  test/controllers/.keep
      create  test/mailers
      create  test/mailers/.keep
      create  test/models
      create  test/models/.keep
      create  test/helpers
      create  test/helpers/.keep
      create  test/integration
      create  test/integration/.keep
      create  test/test_helper.rb
      create  tmp/cache
      create  tmp/cache/assets
      create  vendor/assets/javascripts
      create  vendor/assets/javascripts/.keep
      create  vendor/assets/stylesheets
      create  vendor/assets/stylesheets/.keep
         run  bundle install
Fetching gem metadata from https://rubygems.org/.........
Fetching additional metadata from https://rubygems.org/..
Resolving dependencies...
Using rake 10.2.2
Using i18n 0.6.9
Using json 1.8.1
Using minitest 5.3.1
Using atomic 1.1.16
Using thread_safe 0.3.1
Using tzinfo 1.1.0
Using activesupport 4.1.0.rc2
Using builder 3.2.2
Using erubis 2.7.0
Using actionview 4.1.0.rc2
Using rack 1.5.2
Using rack-test 0.6.2
```

Now, you should have a new folder inside `Bootstrap_Rails_Project` named `TODO`, which was created by the preceding code. Here is the output:

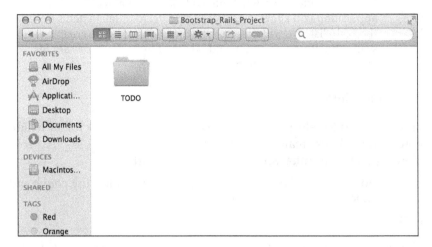

Analyzing folder structure of a Rails application

Let's navigate to the `TODO` folder to check how our application's folder structure looks like:

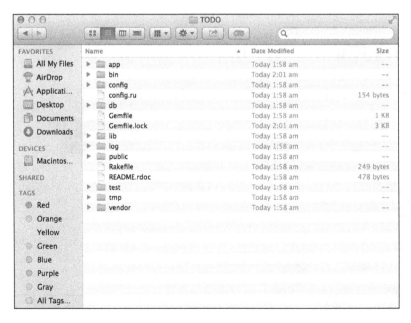

Let me explain to you some of the important folders here:

- The first one is the `app` folder, which we will be focusing on the most throughout this book. All our application's content will be present inside this folder.
- The `assets` folder inside the `app` folder is the location to store all the static files like JavaScript, CSS, and Images. You can take a sneak peek inside them to look at the various files.
- The `controllers` folder handles various requests and responses of the browser.
- The `helpers` folder contains various helper methods both for the `views` and `controllers`.
- The next folder `mailers`, contains all the necessary files to send an e-mail.
- The `models` folder contains files that interact with the database.
- Finally, we have the `views` folder, which contains all the `.erb` files that will be complied to HTML files.

So, let's start the Rails server and check out our application on the browser:

1. Navigate to the TODO folder in the terminal and then type the following command to start a server:

   ```
   rails server
   ```

   You can also use the following command:

   ```
   rails s
   ```

2. You will see that the server is deployed under the port `3000`. So, type the following URL to view the application:

   ```
   http://localhost:3000.
   ```

   You can also use the following URL: `http://0.0.0.0:3000`.

3. If your application is properly set up, you should see the default page of Rails in the browser:

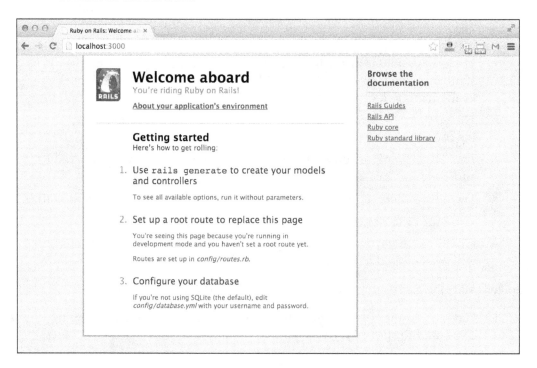

Creating views

We will be using Rails' scaffold method to create models, views, and other necessary files that Rails needs to make our application live. Here's the set of tasks that our application should perform:

- It should list out the pending items
- Every task should be clickable, and the details related to that item should be seen in a new view
- We can edit that item's description and some other details
- We can delete that item

The task looks pretty lengthy, but any Rails developer would know how easy it is to do. We don't actually have to do anything to achieve it. We just have to pass a single scaffold command, and the rest will be taken care of.

Close the Rails server using *Ctrl + C* keys and then proceed as follows:

1. First, navigate to the project folder in the terminal. Then, pass the following command:

   ```
   rails g scaffold todo title:string description:text
   completed:boolean
   ```

   This will create a new model called `todo` that has various fields like title, description, and completed. Each field has a type associated with it.

2. Since we have created a new model, it has to be reflected in the database. So, let's migrate it:

   ```
   rake db:create db:migrate
   ```

   The preceding code will create a new table inside a new database with the associated fields.

3. Let's analyze what we have done. The scaffold command has created many HTML pages or views that are needed for managing the `todo` model. So, let's check out our application. We need to start our server again:

   ```
   rails s
   ```

4. Go to the localhost page `http://localhost:3000` at port number `3000`.

5. You should still see the Rails' default page. Now, type the URL: `http://localhost:3000/todos`.

6. You should now see the application, as shown in the following screenshot:

7. Click on **New Todo**, you will be taken to a form which allows you to fill out various fields that we had earlier created. Let's create our first todo and click on **submit**. It will be shown on the listing page:

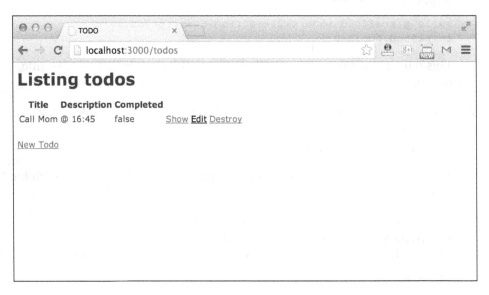

It was easy, wasn't it? We haven't done anything yet. That's the power of Rails, which people are crazy about.

Styling views using CSS

Obviously, the application doesn't look insanely great. The table that has been presented is extremely confusing and needs some CSS styling. So, let's proceed to style our Rails application.

We will use the application's default CSS file to add and modify the styles:

1. Open `Bootstrap_Rails_Project`.

2. Open the `TODO` folder; go to the `app` folder. Navigate to the `assets` folder. There you will find a folder named `stylesheets`. This folder contains all the CSS files of the application.

Currently, you will find three different files: `application.css`, `scaffold.css.scss`, and `todos.css.scss`. The first file is an application level CSS file. Anything you write inside it will be applied to the whole application. The next two files are Sass files. Rails uses SASS to apply styles to the application. These SASS files are compiled in the CSS files and included in the application on the go.

We will be using a normal CSS file without any SASS to apply styles to our Todo application. Let's first proceed and analyze the HTML source code of our application. The screenshot is as follows:

You can see that all the CSS files are loaded alphabetically here. This can be a serious problem where overriding CSS is concerned. We want our CSS file to be at the end. This will allow us to override the application level styles at some places in future.

So, let's rearrange the CSS files here.To do so, follow the given steps:

1. Open the `application.css` file using a text editor. There you can see some code lines with `require_` as their prefix. We need to tweak them a bit in order to get the desired result, as shown here:

2. Let's create a new CSS file named `styles.css` in the same `stylesheets` folder. Now come back to the `application.css` file.

3. Remove the following line from the file:

```
*= require_tree
```

The preceding line was telling Rails to include all the CSS files in alphabetical order.

4. Now, add the following line:

```
*= require 'styles'
```

The preceding line will include `styles.css` in the application. Ensure that `application.css` looks as shown in the following screenshot:

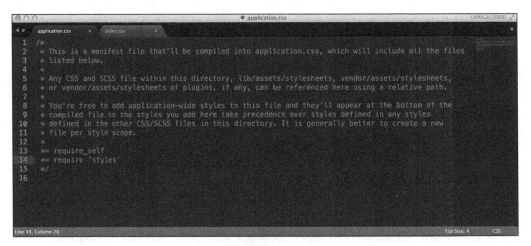

The `require_self` command includes the `application.css` file in the application. If we inspect the HTML source file now, we should see that there are only two CSS files included: `application.css` and `styles.css`. Hence, we are now safe to write CSS styles for the application.

Redesigning the Todo application

In this section, We will write all the CSS files to redesign without the use of any framework. This will help us to better understand the amount of CSS code we have to write at the end for styling simple links and other HTML elements.

We are going to redesign our existing Todo application to something that looks like the following screenshot:

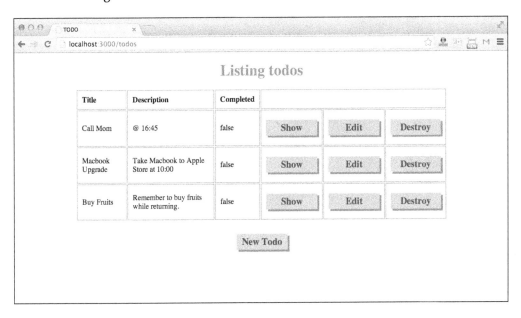

The preceding screenshot displays the redesigned version of the home page. As you can see, the list of TODO activities are now displayed properly in the middle of the screen inside a table-like structure. Even the action links (Show, Edit, and Destroy) have been redesigned to look like 3D buttons. Let's look at the redesigned version:

The preceding screenshot displays the redesigned version of the New Todo page. The form has been redesigned and a background color has been applied to it, as follows:

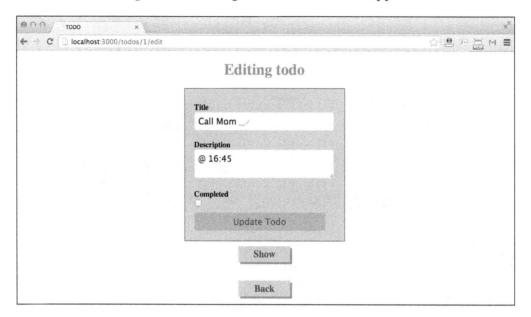

The preceding screenshot shows the redesigned version of the Edit TODO screen, which is the same as the New Todo screen. The only difference here is the auto fill feature that fills the fields as per the data available in the database. The input fields are more spacious with a bigger font size for properly displaying the text contained in them. Let's see the screenshot of the View Todo page:

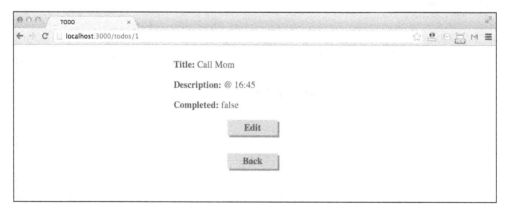

The preceding screenshot displays the redesigned version of the `View Todo` page. We have kept this page simple and clear for better readability. In all the pages, we have centered the content of the website.

Oh! That's lots of designing! Don't worry. We will get through it easily.

It is generally considered as a good practice to organize the designing process before jumping into it. In our Todo application, we have three different views:

- Home page to list out all Todos: This is at `http://localhost:3000/todos`
- New Todo forms and Edit Todo forms: They both are the same view, which is reachable through two different types of URLs
- Show View Todo: It displays particular TODO details

Let's begin by styling the Homepage:

1. Open `styles.css`, which we have recently created. All the styles that we are going to write should be written in this file.

2. We will first clear the browser default margin and padding using the universal selector in CSS (*). So, our CSS for this will be:

```
*{
margin: 0;
padding: 0
}
```

3. Let's style the title of the page first. If you check out the HTML source code of the page, you will see that it is an `H1` element. So, our CSS for this will be:

```
h1{
padding: 20px;
text-align: center;
color: #5093C2;
}
```

The preceding code makes the title appear in the center of the page. It also adds a light blue color to it. We have also created some space around it using the padding property of CSS. Refresh your page to verify it.

4. It's time to decorate the `table` element. Our CSS for it will be:

```
table{
  width: 800px;
  margin: auto;
text-align: center;
}
```

The preceding code makes the table position to the center of the browser. First, we applied a width of 800px to it and then we applied an auto positioned margin to it. Since the browser now knows the width of the table element, it will automatically divide the extra space on each side of it. This will make our table centered to the browser screen. The last property, text-align is used to align the text present inside the table.

5. Let's apply some more styles to the elements present inside the table:

```
td, th{
    padding: 10px;
    border: 1px solid #888888;
}
```

In the preceding CSS code, we have applied styles to the td and th elements of the table element. We created some space around the text using padding. We also applied a border to each cell. It is a solid border of 1px width and color #888888.

6. It's time to design the application's links. We will try to make them appear like a button so that it appears more clickable. Our CSS for it will be:

```
a{
display: block;
text-decoration: none;
width: 100px;
margin: 10px auto;
padding: 5px;
text-align: center;
background: #ccc;
color: #444;
font-size: 20px;
box-shadow: 4px 4px 0px #888;
font-weight: bold;
}
```

Links <a> are inline HTML elements. Hence in the first line, we have made it look like a block-level element using the display property. Now, we can apply width and margin to it. Just like we did to our table element; we will also apply a particular width and make all the links appear centered to their parent elements. We have also applied a padding of 5px to create space around the link text.

To color the links, we applied background to it, and to make the text appear more distinct in this background, we applied a color property to it. We have also played with the shadow of the button to make it appear more 3D.

Make sure to refresh the browser screen to see the changes we are continuously applying. Hope you are enjoying the process of designing the application.

We have finally designed the home screen. The form is still not styled! Let's do it now:

1. Click on the `New Todo` file and let's style it:

```
form{
    width: 300px;
    margin: auto;
    background: #ccc;
    padding: 20px;
    border: 1px solid #444;
}
```

   We applied proper width to the form and made it appear at the center of the screen. We have also given a decent background color to it. Padding and border is also applied to make it look more spacious and flat.

2. Next, we have to design the labels and input fields. If you check out the HTML source of this page, you will see that every label, and its associated input field, is wrapped inside a `div` which has a `field` class. Remember that these classes and the HTML structures are not written by us. These have been autogenerated by Rails. We are just working with the CSS file.

3. Now, we will use the `field` class to apply style to the elements present inside the `New Todo` view. Here we will design the label, input field, and `textarea` element:

```
.field{
    padding: 10px 0;
}

.field label{
        font-weight: bold;
}

.field input, .field textarea{
    padding: 8px;
    border: 1px solid #ccc;
    border-radius: 5px;
    font-size: 18px;
    width: 280px;
}
```

We applied a decent space inside the `field` with `div` element. Here, we have give two different values to the padding property. The first value is for creating spaces to the top and bottom, whereas the next value will be used for the left and right side.

4. Next, we applied style to the label element of the `field` element. We have made it appear bold using the `font-weight` property. Lastly, we gave both the input fields and `textarea` the same set of CSS styles. We made them look spacious using padding. A border property is applied to get rid of the browser default border around the input and textarea elements. We also applied border-radius to make the corners a little rounded. Finally, we fixed the width of both the textarea and input elements so that they appear properly aligned.

5. It's time to design the last element in this HTML page, the `Create Todo` button:

```
.actions input{
    padding: 8px;
    border: 1px solid #CCC;
    border-radius: 5px;
    font-size: 18px;
    width: 280px;
    background: #83B5D8;
    color: #444;
}
```

Most of the CSS styles that we applied here are similar to what we have applied to the input and textarea element. Here, we have added two extra properties, `background` and `color` to make it look different and stand out properly in the form.

6. We have successfully designed the `New Todo` and `Edit Todo` pages. We are now only left with the `Show Todo` page. So, without any further delay, let's first check out the page. Click on the **Show** link.

Most of the content is already styled by us. We are only left with designing the text on this page, the code is as follows:

```
p{
    width: 350px;
    font-size: 20px;
    margin: auto;
    padding: 10px 0;
    color: #444;
```

```
}

p#notice{
  color: #76a3da;
}
```

We applied a fixed width to the p element and made it appear to the center of the screen using the margin property. We also applied a decent font size to them. Now, let's separate them from each other using the margin and padding properties.

This page is also shown after the New Todo or Edit Todo pages with a notice at the top. This element has an id element, which is used to show the status, whether a new todo was successfully created or an existing todo was successfully updated. Using CSS, we have applied style to it. Make sure that you are not giving any space between p and #notice in the preceding CSS code. We are targeting the p tag, which has an id, #notice, so spaces shouldn't be present between the selectors.

Congrats! We have successfully completed designing the whole application.

Challenges in styling a Rails application traditionally

The application which we have created was so basic that we did not write a single line of code for its logic part. We didn't even touch the HTML layout of the application. You have seen how complex the CSS styling can be at some places, such as designing a link. The CSS which we have written here is very poorly organized. We have a target element level selector at many places to apply styles to them. This is considered as a very poor way of designing.

Our CSS code was not segregated into various, smaller parts. All the styles were written directly in one file, styles.css. In the coming chapters, we will see how we can use SASS to apply styles to our Rails applications. Using SASS, we can bring logic to the CSS codes.

We will also overcome the difficulties of styling each and every element in our Rails application using Bootstrap. You will realize how easy it can become for a Non-CSS developer to design a high-end application using Bootstrap. You won't write a single piece of CSS code when using Bootstrap. Its developers have written a bunch of CSS codes for you.

Summary

The main intention of this chapter, was to brief you on how to develop and design a simple Rails application without the help of any CSS frontend frameworks. We manually styled the application by creating an external CSS file `styles.css` and importing it into the application using another CSS file `application.css`. We also discussed the complexities that a novice web designer might face on directly styling the application.

In the next chapter, we will get our hands dirty with Bootstrap. We will learn what it is, and how it can help to design a Rails application quickly. We will also learn how to integrate Bootstrap with the Rails application.

2
Introducing Bootstrap 3

In the last chapter, we learned how to create a simple Rails project, and how to change its default CSS styles. The styling process becomes more difficult if the developer is a newbie and has minimal knowledge of CSS. Bootstrap helps to solve this issue. It gives you access to some of the popular, ready-to-use reusable components such as stylish navigation bars, image containers, popovers, and so on. All you have to do is copy and customize the markup of the component you want to use.

In this chapter, you will understand what Bootstrap is, and how it is important for a Rails developer. We will see how to download and use Bootstrap in our Rails projects. We will again create the same Todo application in this chapter and apply Bootstrap styles to it.

In this chapter, we will cover:

- What is Bootstrap?
- Installing Bootstrap in a Rails project

What is Bootstrap?

Bootstrap is a complete frontend framework that helps in developing web applications without having to worry about its frontend. If you are a developer and your main focus is to showcase the power of your application without putting any efforts on CSS designing, then Bootstrap is for you. It allows developers to select from a range of popular reusable HTML components that are previously developed and styled by Bootstrap.

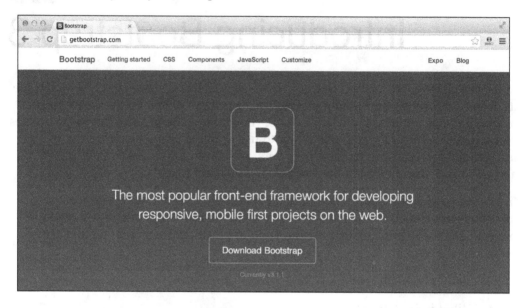

Let's imagine a situation. Thomas is a Rails developer. He creates a powerful e-commerce shopping system using Rails. The system has many features which are normally expected from a shopping website. Thomas puts his extra effort on securing the application, and he made the system ready to use. Then comes the time when Thomas has to finally represent this application to venture capitalists to get some funding in order to start his project. But wait, Thomas did nothing to make his application presentable. His application contains only basic HTML markup with almost negligible CSS styling in it. Will his application make an impact?

The answer is, definitely not. Though Thomas was able to create a robust Rails application, it lacked presentation ability. His lack of proper CSS knowledge was the main reason that debarred him from creating a powerful impact for his project.

It is always important to balance both the frontend and backend capability for every developer. If you can't represent your application in a presentable manner, then it is definitely of no use. There might be some developers who will go forward after learning a lesson from a similar event, as described in the preceding example. They will try hard and learn web designing using CSS irrespective of whether they have interest in that area. By doing this, they are forgetting that designing is a completely different field from what they were previously doing. It is the work of UX/UI developers.

Bootstrap developers have written many CSS definitions that can be directly plugged into our projects to represent it. It is also an open source project which is licensed under MIT. This gives you freedom to use it on any type of projects without worrying about the licensing issues. Why should we reinvent the wheel, when someone has already done the job for us? Developers who are focused on rapid application development should consider using Bootstrap in their every project.

Bootstrap is not limited to just providing better CSS components to the developers. It is a **mobile first** framework. This means that anything you write in your application using Bootstrap will be compatible even on smaller mobile devices. Bootstrap-powered applications can scale beautifully from extremely small devices like iPhones to larger displays like Retina displays. It helps you to write a single codebase and use it everywhere. With the advancement of technology, even native iOS and Android applications can be written using HTML, CSS, and JavaScript today. They are called **Hybrid applications** that are ported into the native platforms using tools like PhoneGap. Imagine that your Rails application is being used in all types of devices like mobiles, smart TVs, tablets, and even desktop screens. Awesome! Isn't it?

Installing Bootstrap in a Rails project

Bootstrap is simply a package of CSS, JavaScript, and font files. You must be confused why we used the term installing with Bootstrap here. Well, there are two different ways of using Bootstrap in Rails. The first one is to directly copy the Bootstrap files at proper places in the Rails project. The second one is the *Bootstrap Sass way*. It is because of the second way that we used the term installing. It also comes as a gemset that can be bundle installed in any Rails project. We will explore both the ways in detail in this section.

There's also a third way, using Bootstrap files from CDN, which is the simplest of all. We will explore this at the end.

Placing Bootstrap files in a Rails project

This is the first method of using Bootstrap in Rails. Many Rails developers get this method wrong. Placing the Bootstrap files properly is very important to activate Bootstrap. Follow these steps to place Bootstrap files:

1. Let's create a new Rails project. This time we will name it as the `Rails_Bootstrap_Project` command, as follows:

   ```
   rails new Rails_Bootstrap_Project
   ```

   As usual, the preceding code will run various other commands and will take some time to complete. We will not discuss about various folders that are created inside this Rails project, as this was already covered in the previous chapter.

2. Let's create a new model in Rails called `todos` using the scaffolding command, as follows:

   ```
   rails g scaffold todos title:string description:text
   completed:boolean
   ```

3. Let's also make this change in the database by using the migrate command, as follows:

   ```
   rake db:migrate
   ```

4. You should get a successful migration message. It's time to start the server and check out the Todo application.

   ```
   rails s
   ```

You can now visit `http://localhost:3000/todos` and click on **New Todo**. The application should work, and you will get a screenshot, as follows:

Once the installation is complete, we will get a folder called `Rails_Bootstrap_Project` with lots of files inside it. If you are a Rails developer, you will definitely be tempted to jump directly into it. Let's keep this project as it is for the time being and proceed to download Bootstrap from its official website. The steps are:

1. Go to `http://getbootstrap.com` and click on the **Download Bootstrap** button. It will take you to another page with three different options available.

2. Select the first button which simply says **Download Bootstrap**. A zipped package will start downloading.

3. After the downloading is over, extract all the files. You can see three different folders present inside the default Bootstrap package, `css`, `js`, and `fonts`. We need to get all these files properly in our Rails project in order to make Bootstrap work.

Every Bootstrap package comes with a standard set of files. The `css` folder contains four different CSS files. The first two CSS files are: `bootstrap.css` and `bootstrap.min.css`. Both of these files are exactly the same, except the way they are created. Here, `bootstrap.css` is a document version whereas `bootstrap.min.css` is a minified version. You will not find any comments or proper indentation in the minified version. A minified version is good for using in projects that are ready for production, as it is smaller in size.

The next two files, `bootstrap.theme.css` and `bootstrap.theme.min.css`, are theme files from Bootstrap. Bootstrap has created its own theme file to override its own default style on various components. They are completely optional. Personally, I have never used them. These two theme files are also exactly the same. The first one is a documented version while the second is a minified version.

Moving on to the `js` folder of the Bootstrap package, we will find two different JavaScript files: `bootstrap.js` and `bootstrap.min.js`. Again, these two files are exactly similar in nature. The former is a documented version while the latter is a minified version. This is the main Bootstrap JavaScript file. There are many components like navigation bar which depend on this file to function properly. Bootstrap's JavaScript components depend on jQuery. We do not get jQuery, out of the box, in the Bootstrap's package. But, it is necessary to include in our application. Generally, all the Rails projects include jQuery in them. Hence, we don't have to include it separately.

Bootstrap comes with a set of icons that can be used in our Rails application. These icons are called **Glyphicons**. Unlike other icons which are images, these icons are fonts. All the icons are present in various font files inside the `fonts` folder of the Bootstrap package.

Now that we have taken a walkthrough of all the files in the Bootstrap package, let's start importing them in our Rails application using the following steps:

1. Let's move the CSS file first. Copy bootstrap.min.css from the CSS folder and place it in the stylesheets folder of the Rails application by navigating to vendor/assets/stylesheets:

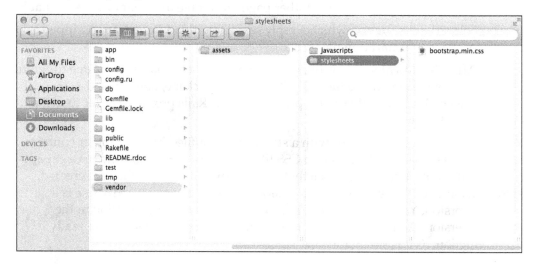

2. Next, copy bootstrap.min.js from the js folder and paste it in the javascripts folder of the Rails application by navigating to vendor/assets/javascripts:

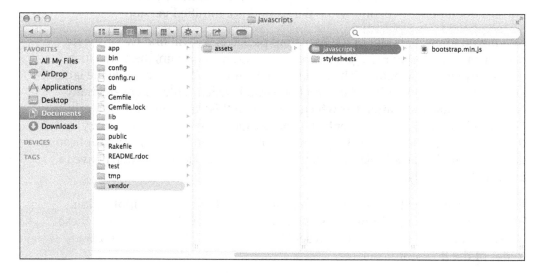

3. Copy the complete `fonts` folder and place it in the `assets` file under `vendor` folder:

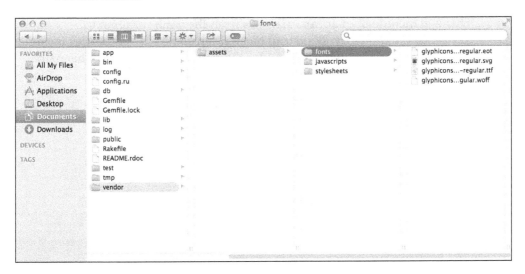

We have all the Bootstrap files in the `vendors/assets` folder now. It's time to link them from the default Rails CSS and JavaScript files.

4. Open the file `application.css` in the `stylesheets` folder by navigating to `app/assets/stylesheets`:

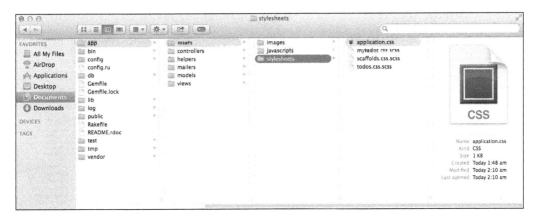

5. Put the following line into the application of `.css` file:

```
*= require bootstrap.min
```

This will include `bootstrap.min.css` from the `vendor/assets/stylesheets` directory. Bootstrap has written some CSS properties inside `bootstrap.min.css`, which provides the path to the font files. This path won't work here. We need to override it inside the `application.css` file.

6. Paste the following lines into `application.css`:

```
@font-face {
  font-family: 'Glyphicons Halflings';
  src: url('../assets/glyphicons-halflings-regular.eot');
  src: url('../assets/glyphicons-halflings-
    regular.eot?#iefix') format('embedded-opentype'),
  url('../assets/glyphicons-halflings-regular.woff')
    format('woff'),
  url('../assets/glyphicons-halflings-regular.ttf')
    format('truetype'),
  url('../assets/glyphicons-halflings-regular.
    svg#glyphicons_halflingsregular') format('svg');
}
```

7. We are done with linking the Bootstrap's CSS files. Next, we need to link the Bootstrap's JavaScript file.

   Open the `application.js` file from `app/assets/javascripts` directory:

8. Put the following line into the application of the `.js` file:

```
//= require bootstrap.min
```

This will link the `bootstrap.min.js` file from the `javascripts` folder by navigating to `vendor/assets/javascripts`.

9. Now it's done! Yes, we have successfully implemented Bootstrap in our Rails application. Restart the server and open the Todo application that we have created. You will see some minor changes to the application's appearances:

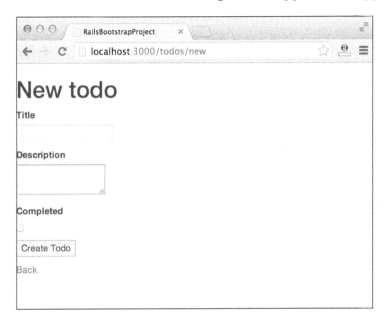

The new screenshot has a bolder and clean font. Bootstrap uses browser reset which clears all the default browser styles. Hence, there's no gap between the elements and the browser window. This helps to properly define the CSS and also assures that your design looks the same in all kinds of browsers.

This was all about injecting Bootstrap's static files directly into a Rails project. Let's take a look at some other methods.

Bootstrap – the Sass way

Bootstrap also supports Sass. It comes as a gemfile that can be directly installed in the Rails application. We will first install Bootstrap as a gem and then try to understand why it is better this way:

1. Let's create another project called `Rails_Bootstrap_Sass_Project`:

    ```
    rails new Rails_Bootstrap_Sass_Project
    ```

2. After the installation is complete, open `Gemfile` which is present inside the home directory of the application folder.

3. You can see lots of gem dependencies mentioned in this file. We need to add another gem dependency which is `bootstrap-sass`. Add the following line in this file too:

```
gem 'bootstrap-sass', '~> 3.1.1'
```

The above command will install Bootstrap 3.1.1, which is the latest version at the time of writing this book. You can also specify other versions, as per availability.

4. It's time to bundle install this project again. Go to the terminal and navigate to the `Rails_Bootstrap_Sass_Project` folder in it. Then, type the following command:

```
bundle install
```

5. This will fetch the `gem bootstrap-sass`, and include it in the project. Let's create a model called `todos` using the scaffolding command, as shown:

```
rails g scaffold todos title:string description:text
completed:boolean
```

6. Also complete the database migration using the rake command, as shown:

```
rake db:migrate
```

7. Once the migration is done, we will link the Bootstrap's `css` and `js` file from Rails' default `css` and `javascript` files.

Open the `todos.css.scss` file which is present inside the `stylesheets` folder by navigating to the `app/assets/stylesheets` folder. Place the following line in it:

```
@import "bootstrap";
```

8. Next, open the `application.js` file in the `javascripts` folder by navigating to `app/assets/javascripts`. Insert the following line in it:

```
//= require bootstrap
```

We are done! Simple, wasn't it?

If you run this project, you can see Bootstrap's fonts and resets have been applied to the default application.

Bootstrap through CDN

Content delivery network (CDN) is a way of hosting popular libraries in the cloud and allows developers to directly access these files whenever needed. There are some of the popular CDN service providers like Google Hosted Libraries (`https://developers.google.com/speed/libraries/devguide`), cdnjs (`http://cdnjs.com/`), CloudFlare (`http://www.cloudflare.com/`), and others.

Bootstrap also comes with a CDN support. They have hosted both the CSS and JavaScript file in their own cloud servers. Let's try to use CDN in a Rails project this time, using the following steps:

1. Create a new Rails project called `Rails_Bootstrap_CDN_project`:

   ```
   rails new Rails_Bootstrap_CDN_project
   ```

2. Once the project is created, make a new model called todos using scaffolding:

   ```
   rails g scaffold todos title:string description:text
   completed:boolean
   ```

3. Do the database migration using the following command:

   ```
   rails db:migrate
   ```

4. Once all the above steps are successfully completed, go to the newly created folder `Rails_Bootstrap_CDN_project`. Go to `app/assets/stylesheets` and open the `application.css` file.

5. We need to import Bootstrap's CSS file from its CDN in this file. Hence, paste the following lines in it:

   ```
   @import "//netdna.bootstrapcdn.com/bootstrap/3.1.1/css/bootstrap.
   min.css"
   ```

6. Next, we have to include Bootstrap's JavaScript file from its CDN into our main view. Go to `app/views/layouts` and open the `application.html.erb` file. Paste the following line either just above the `</head>` tag or inside the body just above the `</body>` tag.

   ```
   <script src="//netdna.bootstrapcdn.com/bootstrap/3.1.1/js/
   bootstrap.min.js">
   </script>
   ```

It's done! You have successfully imported all the Bootstrap files into your Rails package. Go ahead, run the server and check out the app. It should have Bootstrap's styles applied to it.

Summary

Out of all the methods of importing/installing Bootstrap in a Rails project, I would definitely suggest you to go with the Sass way. Developers familiar with Sass should definitely go for it.

Sass allows developers to completely customize Bootstrap's default styles and behavior. As we will progress with this book, we will see how to customize Bootstrap through Sass. Sass brings modularity to the CSS world. It brings the programming capability in it. You can use variables, functions, inheritance, and so on using Sass.

CDN is another better alternative but is very risky. CDN is generally blocked in many secure networks. In such cases, your application will load without any Bootstrap files. CDN also reduces the performance of the web app by sending an extra request to a different network. Hope you have got a fair idea of what Bootstrap is through this chapter. It is an extremely useful framework that enforces rapid development by the use of its HTML and CSS components. In the coming chapters, we will see how to use some of the popular Bootstrap components in the Rails applications. We will see how easy it is to create a highly responsive Rails application using Bootstrap.

3
Powering a Rails App with Bootstrap's Grid System

We now have a good knowledge of what Bootstrap is, and how we can get it installed in our projects. With this chapter, we will understand the what can be done part of Bootstrap.

Grid system is an integral part of the Bootstrap framework. You won't be able to make a responsive website/application without properly understanding Bootstrap's grid system. By responsive, I mean an application that works and looks perfect in devices of all sizes.

This is the generation of Hybrid applications! Developers want to write the code once and make it accessible from all the devices. To do this, they have to first make their web application responsive. Bootstrap helps in creating a responsive website using one of its most popular features called **grid system**.

In this chapter, we will first understand Bootstrap's grid system and then proceed to use it in our first application called Online Packt Shopping. We will try to use this same app in the rest of book.

In this chapter, we will cover:

- What is Bootstrap's grid system?
- Implementing Bootstrap's Grid System in Rails application

What is Bootstrap's grid system?

When we first think about grids, we imagine the intersection of vertical and horizontal lines that create grids. That's what's happening here too. Bootstrap's grid system contains rows equivalent to horizontal lines, and columns equivalent to vertical lines. When these rows and columns meet, they create grids, which can be used to fill some content in our webpage. Simple, isn't it?

One of the biggest advantages of using Bootstrap's grid system is that it is responsive. Unlike HTML tables, Bootstrap's grid system is flexible and adjusts itself properly in the smaller screens as well. The size of the grids in Bootstrap isn't fixed. They change as per the size of the device's screen. Hence, the content is rearranged, as per the space available.

Most developers fail to understand the grid system properly and hence they fail to achieve a responsive web design. In this section, we will first create a static non-Rails webpage showcasing how to create Bootstrap's Grid System, and then we will use it in our Rails application.

Let's create a folder called `Responsive_website_static` anywhere in the system. Then, create an HTML file called `index.html`. We will use Bootstrap's CDN link to import Bootstrap's CSS and JavaScript codes inside the webpage. Now, open the `index.html` file and then paste the following basic HTML layout into it:

```
<!DOCTYPE html>
<html lang="en">
  <head>f
    <meta charset="utf-8">
    <meta http-equiv="X-UA-Compatible" content="IE=edge">
    <meta name="viewport" content="width=device-width,
      initial-scale=1">
    <title>Responsive_website_static</title>
    <!-- Bootstrap -->
    <link rel="stylesheet" href="http://maxcdn.bootstrapcdn.com/
      bootstrap/3.2.0/css/bootstra. min.css">
  </head>
  <body>
    <h1>Hello, world!</h1>
    <!-- jQuery (necessary for Bootstrap's JavaScript plugins) -->
    <script src="https://ajax.googleapis.com/ajax/libs/jquery/
      1.11.1/jquery.min.js">
    </script>
    <!-- Include all compiled plugins (below), or include
      individual files as needed -->
```

```
    <script src="http://maxcdn.bootstrapcdn.com/bootstrap/3.2.0/
      js/bootstrap.min.js">
    </script>
  </body>
</html>
```

The above markup is as per Bootstrap's recommended markup. You can see that it has got some additional meta tags also. These meta tags are used to render the webpage properly in all kinds of devices. The `UTF-8` charset is used to tell the browser that your webpage contains some `unicode` characters.

The next meta tag with the `http-equiv="X-UA-Compatible"` and `content="IE=edge"` attributes is used for Internet Explorer. Sometimes, Internet Explorer switches to the compatible mode instead of using its best mode available. Hence, this tag tells Internet Explorer to use its best mode when rendering your website.

The next meta tag is a `viewport` tag. It tells the browser to scale and fit the webpage to the whole screen in mobile devices.

Instead of downloading the Bootstrap files from its browser, we have used the CDN links to link to the Bootstrap's CSS and JavaScript files. Since Bootstrap also depends on jQuery, we have also used the CDN link of the jQuery file.

Finally, we have an `<h1>` tag to display the message **Hello World** on the webpage. So, let's open it in the browser and check whether all the files have been properly loaded. The webpage should now look like the following screenshot:

If you are using Google Chrome, you can easily check whether all the CDN files are loaded properly. Right-click anywhere on the webpage, and select the inspect element. Many web developer tool tabs will appear below the screen. Select the **Network** tab and reload the page. In the **Status Text** column, you will see many response codes against each resource name. If none of the response codes fail, then all the files are loaded properly.

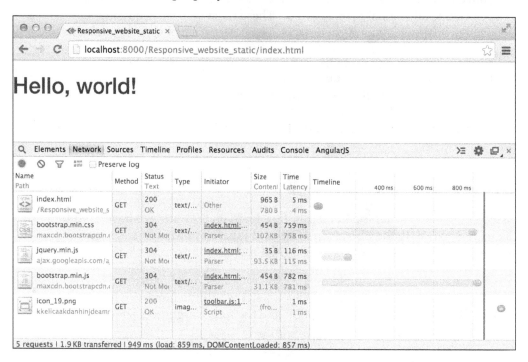

Before we start filling any content inside the webpage, we need to create a container. This will be used to wrap all the webpage content and center it to the browser screen. There are two different container classes in Bootstrap: "container" and "container-fluid" The first class, "container", has a fixed width and centers itself to the browser window. The second class, "container-fluid", is a full width container. It spans from the left edge to the right edge of the browser window. So, let's define a container inside index.html and move the Hello World message inside it:

```
<div class="container">
  <h1>Hello World</h1>
</div>
```

The following screenshot shows the output:

You can see how it has moved the message towards the center. It will be more clearly visible if we apply a background to the container. So, let's write an inline CSS to the container markup:

```
<div class="container" style="background: cyan">
  <h1>Hello World</h1>
</div>
```

Here's the output of the preceding code:

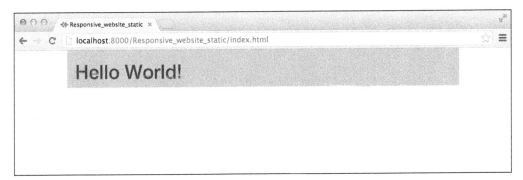

You should always define a container before using Bootstrap's Grid System. We can now proceed to define rows. To define a row, we have to use a class called row. So, let's proceed and create a row inside the container:

```
<div class="container">
  <div class="row">
  </div>
</div>
```

Creating a row is a way of telling Bootstrap that you want to use its grid system. It's time to layout vertical columns inside the above row. A single column in Bootstrap will occupy all the space inside the row. Creating two columns will divide the row's space into two equal halves. Hence, the more columns you create, the row's space will be divided equally. Bootstrap's grid system scales up to 12 columns. If you create more than 12 columns, the remaining columns will be moved automatically to a new row. So, let's first create a single column:

```
<div class="container" style="background: cyan">
  <div class="row">
    <div class="col-xs-12" style="background: green">
      <h1>Hello World</h1>
    </div>
  </div>
</div>
```

Let's take a look at the output:

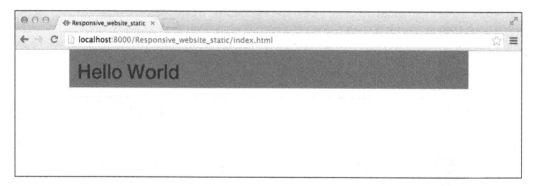

A column in the Bootstrap grid system is declared using the amount of columns it will span across. If you want to create a single column, you need it to span across 12 Bootstrap columns. Hence, we get the class `"col-xs-12"`. If you want to create two columns, you have to use the class `"col-xs-6"`. This will make each column span across six Bootstrap columns. So, let's proceed and create two columns in the preceding markup:

```
<div class="container" style="background: cyan">
    <div class="row">
      <div class="col-xs-6" style="background: green">
        <h1>Hello</h1>
      </div>
```

```
    <div class="col-xs-6" style="background: red">
      <h1>World</h1>
    </div>
  </div>
</div>
```

Let's take a look at the output:

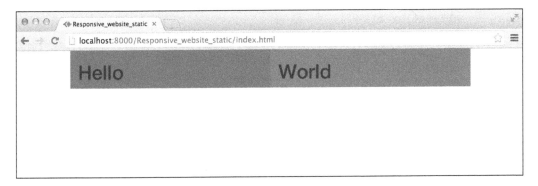

Bootstrap has defined classes for devices of different sizes. In the preceding examples, we have been using the classes such as `"col-xs-*"`. Here the letters *xs* stand for extra-small devices and the devices above that range. Hence a class, `"col-xs-"` will create a column of size 12 Bootstrap columns in all types of devices starting from extra-small devices. There are four different types of Bootstrap classes for four different sizes of devices:

- `Extra-Small Devices ".col-xs-*"`: These devices have a screen size less than 768 px
- `Small Devices ".col-sm-*"`: These devices have a screen size less than 992 px and larger than or equal to 786 px
- `Medium Devices ".col-md-*"`: These devices have a screen size less than 1200 px and larger than and equal to 992 px
- `Large Devices ".col-lg-*"`: These devices have a screen size larger than 1200 px

For instance, if you are defining columns, keeping in mind medium devices greater than or equal to 992 px, then these columns will look the same even in larger devices greater than or equal to 992 px 1200 px. They will be stacked on top of each other in small devices smaller than 992 px and extra-small devices 768 px. Hence, if you define columns for extra-small devices, then they will look the same in all kinds of devices.

Using Bootstrap, you can also dynamically change the number of columns in different devices. For example, using the classes `"col-xs-4"` and `"col-sm-6"` together will make a column span across four Bootstrap columns in extra-small devices, and six Bootstrap columns in small devices. The steps are as follows:

```
<div class="container" style="background: cyan">
  <div class="row">
    <div class="col-xs-12 col-sm-6" style="background: green">
      <h1>Hello</h1>
    </div>
    <div class="col-xs-12 col-sm-6" style="background: red">
      <h1>World</h1>
    </div>
  </div>
</div>
```

Let's take a look at the output:

The preceding screenshot shows the webpage in extra-small devices. The browser renders one column per row because of the class `"col-xs-12"`.

Hopefully, now you have got an idea of how Bootstrap's columns are named. So, let's proceed to another important concept in Bootstrap's grid system, nesting columns.

Nesting columns

In Bootstrap, it is possible to define columns within columns. To do so, you need to declare a new row within a column markup and then proceed to create columns within it. Let's modify the previous code to test nested columns:

```
<div class="container" style="background: cyan">
  <div class="row">
    <div class="col-xs-12 col-sm-6" style="background: green">
      <h1>Hello</h1>
      <div class="row">
        <div class="col-xs-6" style="background: orange">
          <h2>PACKT</h2>
        </div>
        <div class="col-xs-6" style="background: grey">
          <h2>PUBLISHING</h2>
        </div>
      </div>
    </div>
    <div class="col-xs-12 col-sm-6" style="background: red">
      <h1>World</h1>
    </div>
  </div>
</div>
```

Let's take a look at the output:

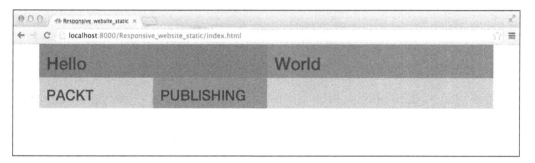

In the preceding screenshot, you can clearly see that we have created two different columns within the first column. Since the second column doesn't have any nested columns in it, the background color (cyan) of the main container is now visible to us. This way you can create as many nesting columns as you want.

Implementing Bootstrap's grid system in a Rails application

It's time to finally use the Grid system in our Rails application. As stated earlier, we will create an application called Online Packt Shopping. We will use grid system in this chapter and create a CRUD app for products. We will continue developing this app throughout this book as we learn Bootstrap's different features.

So, let's proceed and create a Rails application called Online Packt Shopping.

```
rails new OnlinePacktShopping
```

Once the application is created, you should navigate inside the newly created folder and start the Rails server to test if the application is properly installed. So, let's do it using the following command:

```
cd /OnlinePacktShopping
```

```
rails server
```

Access the webpage at `http://localhost:3000`. It should show the default Rails app **Welcome Board**.

Our product will have the following four attributes:

- Name
- Featured Image
- Description
- Price

So, let's scaffold accordingly

Now, we will scaffold and generate a product model with the following command:

```
rails generate scaffold Product name:string featImage:string
description:text price:decimal
```

This command will create a model named **NewProduct** and its associated attributes. You need to migrate the newly created model to the database. You can do so using the rake command, which is as follows:

```
rake db:migrate
```

Once this is done successfully, run the server and open: `http://localhost:3000/products`. You should see an empty products listing page:

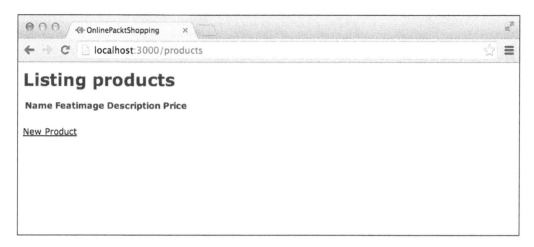

We have to first include Bootstrap in this application. For that, we will use the CDN method, as described in *Chapter 2: Introducing Bootstrap 3* in the section *Installing Bootstrap in a Rails project*.

Once you have included Bootstrap in your application, you can reload the preceding webpage and see the CSS reset the Bootstrap applies on the HTML elements. You can also see that the font has changed from `Times New Roman` to `Open Sans`. So, let's take a look at the output:

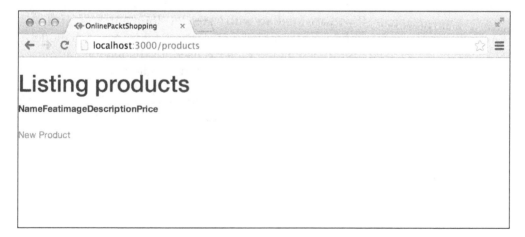

We will follow all the steps, as discussed in the previous section. First, we need to define a container for our application. Open `application.html.erb`, which is present in app/views/layouts.

We need to wrap `<%= yield %>` inside the Bootstrap container markup:

```
<div class="container">
  <%= yield %>
</div>
```

Let's take a look at the output:

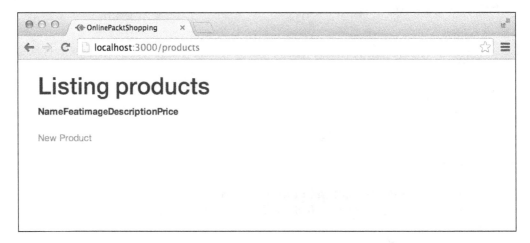

Next, we need to change the way the content appears on this page. We don't need a table to list our products. We will use Bootstrap's grid system to display the products beautifully in a responsive grid layout.

Open `index.html.erb` which is present inside the `products` folder by navigating to `app/views/products`. If you are familiar with Rails development, you must know that there's a separate folder present inside the `views` folder for each model. The `index.html.erb` file inside each model folder is used for displaying various models. Go ahead and delete everything which is present inside this file.

First, we need a page header that tells the users what the page is displaying. So, let's create a page header using Bootstrap's "`.page-header`" class. Insert the following code in `index.html.erb`:

```
<div class="page-header">
  <h3>All Products</h3>
</div>
```

Next, we need to create a row for displaying the products. Hence, update the markup and add the following:

```
<div class="row">
</div>
```

Now, we will create columns inside this row. For our application, we want the following features in our layout:

- Columns in extra-small mobile devices

- Columns in small mobile devices

- Columns in medium devices

- Columns in large devices

Hence, the combination which we will use to define our column is `"col-xs-12 col-sm-6 col-md-4 col-lg-3"`. Let's proceed and update the preceding row markup with a single column:

```
<div class="row">
  <div class="col-xs-12 col-sm-6 col-md-4 col-lg-3">
  </div>
</div>
```

We will now loop this column markup for each product. Hence, we need to update our markup as following:

```
<div class="row">
  <% @products.each do |product| %>
  <div class="col-xs-12 col-sm-6 col-md-4 col-lg-3">
  </div>
  <% end %>
</div>
```

Now, we need to fill this column with the product details:

```
<div class="row">
  <% @products.each do |product| %>
  <div class="col-xs-12 col-sm-6 col-md-4 col-lg-3 text-center">
    <h2><%= product.name %></h2>
    <img class="img-responsive" src=<%=asset_path
      product.featImage %>/>
    <p><%= product.description %></p>
    <h4>$<%= product.price %></h4>
```

```
      <%= link_to 'Show', product, :class=>"btn btn-primary" %>
   </div>
   <% end %>
</div>
```

In the preceding code, I am looping through the `product` object to repeatedly print the same markup, but with a different data. For each product, I am printing its name using the `<h2>` tag, an image using, `<img>` tag, product description in a `<p>` tag, product price in the `<h4>` tag, and finally the link to the product page using `link_to`.

You can see, that while printing the data in HTML tags, I have also added some additional classes. These classes carry some CSS styles associated with them that are written by Bootstrap. For example, adding a class `"img-responsive"` to an `<img>` tag will make the image fit to the size of the grid, irrespective of the size of the image. I have also used the combination of classes `btn` and `btn-success` which are used for the `<a>` and `<button>` tags. These classes give links a fancy button look. We will learn more about these classes in subsequent chapters.

Let's proceed and check out how this page will look once we have filled data in our database using the `New Product` page:

The preceding screenshot is the desktop view.

The preceding screenshot is a medium-sized device view. This will be the view in most of the tablets in the market, the output for this is:

You can mark that the number of columns is reducing, as per our design requirement. The preceding image shows the layout in smaller devices. The following screenshot shows the view for extra-small devices:

You can see that the layout has changed to single-column design in extra-small devices.

There's still a thing missing in this page, a link to add a new product. Let's place a nice fancy New Product page right-aligned with the page header. An update page header markup is as follows:

```
<div class="page-header">
  <%= link_to 'New Product', new_product_path,
    :class=>"btn btn-success pull-right" %>
  <h3>All Products</h3>
</div>
```

The webpage should now look like:

You must be wondering how I pulled the New Product button to the right side of the page. If you see the markup properly, I have used an additional Bootstrap class named `pull-right`. These classes are called helper classes in Bootstrap. There are many helper classes in Bootstrap, we will learn more about them as we proceed with the book.

Summary

In this chapter, we understood Bootstrap's Grid System and created two different types of projects: a static demo webpage and an online shopping Rails app. We saw how to use the Grid system, and make our homepage responsive to various sizes of devices. There are still many pages left unstyled in the current app: `add product` page, `edit product` page, and `single product` page. We will use Bootstrap to style them in subsequent chapters.

In the next chapter, we will understand various typography support from Bootstrap, play with beautiful Bootstrap buttons, and do more with images using Bootstrap.

4

Using Bootstrap's Typography, Buttons, and Images in a Rails Application

Styling a website's text, images, and links is a very important part of any web design. In the preceding chapter, we saw how to define a proper layout of a website using Bootstrap's grid system. In this chapter, we are going to focus more on styling the website's content like text, links, and images.

Bootstrap comes with many default styles for various HTML elements. For example, it comes with default styles for anchor tags, heading tags, ordered and unordered lists, and many more. These styles are applied using particular classes defined by Bootstrap.

Bootstrap focuses on rapid web development. So, when developers with little knowledge of web designing start using Bootstrap, it doesn't let them down. These smaller default styles of Bootstrap will help you get rid of browser default styles of many HTML elements.

In this chapter, we will cover the following topics:

- Styling typography
- Creating Bootstrap buttons
- Styling images in Bootstrap

Setting up

In this chapter, we are going to use the same static website setup, `Responsive_website_static`, that was created in *Chapter 3, Powering a Rails App with Bootstrap's Grid System*. Copy the folder `Responsive_website_static` and rename it as `Bootstrap_default_styles`. Open the `index.html` file and remove everything from the `<body>` tag, except Bootstrap's JavaScript. Change the title of the page to `Bootstrap default styles`. Your `index.html` file should now have the following content:

```html
<!DOCTYPE html>
  <html lang="en">
    <head>
      <meta charset="utf-8">
      <meta http-equiv="X-UA-Compatible" content="IE=edge">
      <meta name="viewport" content="width=device-width,
        initial-scale=1">
      <title>Bootstrap default styles</title>
      <!-- Bootstrap -->
      <link rel="stylesheet" href="http://maxcdn.bootstrapcdn.com/
        bootstrap/3.2.0/css/bootstrap.min.css">
    </head>
  <body>
    <!-- jQuery (necessary for Bootstrap's JavaScript plugins) -->
    <script src="https://ajax.googleapis.com/ajax/libs/jquery/
      1.11.1/jquery.min.js"></script>
    <!-- Include all compiled plugins (below), or include
      individual files as needed -->
    <script src="http://maxcdn.bootstrapcdn.com/bootstrap/
      3.2.0/js/bootstrap.min.js"></script>
  </body>
</html>
```

As you learned in *Chapter 3, Powering a Rails App with Bootstrap's Grid System*, you should place a `div` container inside the `body` tag to wrap all of the website's content and place them properly at the center of the screen. So, let's create a container using the following markup:

```html
<div class="container">
</div>
```

Styling typography

When we talk about typography, we mean heading tags, paragraph tags, inline text elements, proper alignment, text transformations, and any text on your webpage.

Bootstrap comes with default styles for all the heading tags starting from <h1> to <h6>. If you want to create a heading tag in your HTML page, you can directly put the heading tag without any classes. Let's have a look at an example. Insert the following HTML elements inside the static website that was created previously:

```
<div class="container">
    <h1>Let's save the Earth.</h1>
    <h2>Let's save the Earth.</h2>
    <h3>Let's save the Earth.</h3>
    <h4>Let's save the Earth.</h4>
    <h5>Let's save the Earth.</h5>
    <h6>Let's save the Earth.</h6>
</div>
```

The output of the preceding code will look like this in the browser:

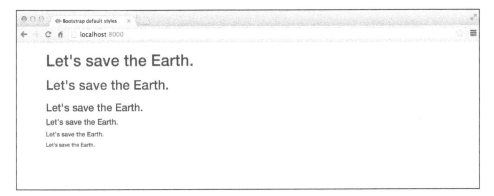

There might be scenarios when you don't use a heading tag, but are able to achieve the same default style with some other HTML elements. Bootstrap will help you to do this. You can use the class ".h1" through ".h6" to get the desired typography style. Let's remove all the heading tags in the preceding example and use paragraph tags instead. This time, we will use Bootstrap's heading classes to get the same style:

```
<div class="container">
    <p class="h1">Let's save the Earth.</p>
    <p class="h2">Let's save the Earth.</p>
    <p class="h3">Let's save the Earth.</p>
```

```
    <p class="h4">Let's save the Earth.</p>
    <p class="h5">Let's save the Earth.</p>
    <p class="h6">Let's save the Earth.</p>
</div>
```

The preceding markup will look like this in the browser:

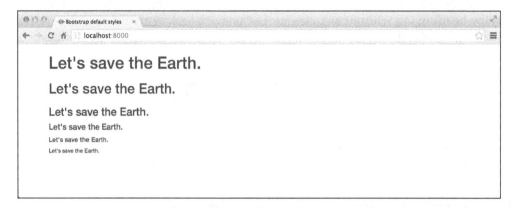

It's time to add a subtitle to the heading tag. Subtitles are very useful when you want to display a short tag line for your website. In Bootstrap, we will use the HTML tag "<small>" to add a subtitle within any heading tag of your choice. A small tag is an inline tag used for the same pupose in raw HTML as well. Take the following code as an example:

```
<div class="container">
<h1>Save Earth <small>A PACKT Publishing Initiative.</small></h1>
</div>
```

The output will look as follows:

You can see how the small tag appears relatively smaller, as compared to the heading tag content, even though they are present in the same tag.

Let's talk about styling the paragraph tags. Bootstrap applies a default size of 14px to all the paragraph tags. You don't have to use any class for applying Bootstrap's style to a paragraph tag. Let's check out an example. I have inserted two dummy paragraphs in the preceding markup. Let's apply the code:

```
<p>
    Lorem ipsum dolor sit amet, consectetur adipiscing elit.
        In fringilla dictum libero, vel placerat lorem elementum
            tristique.
</p>
<p>
    Pellentesque laoreet ipsum libero, eu commodo ligula semper
        in. Fusce vitae feugiat lorem. Morbi tempor, nunc in
            auctor blandit, nibh purus scelerisque sem,…..
</p>
```

The output will look like this in the browser:

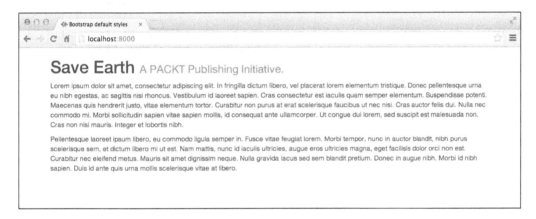

You can even tweak a paragraph tag to stand out among the rest of the paragraph tags in the webpage using the .lead class. Let's add this class to the first paragraph in the preceding markup and checkout the difference that it creates:

```
<p class="lead">
    Lorem ipsum dolor sit amet, consectetur adipiscing elit.
        In fringilla dictum libero, vel placerat lorem elementum
            tristique.
</p>
```

The output will look as follows:

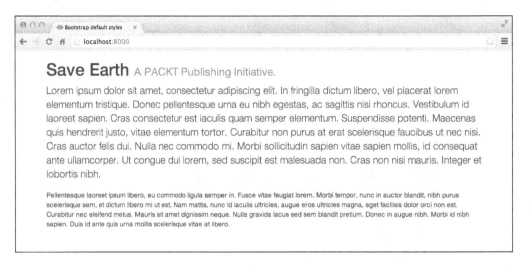

Bootstrap even allows you to highlight text in a paragraph using the `<mark>` tag. I have added the `<mark>` tag in the paragraph, which gets highligted in the preceding markup, and got the following result:

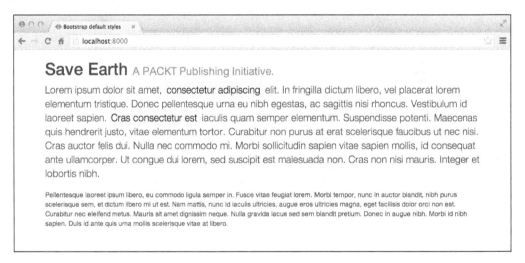

Some other typography features are as follows:

- You can strikethrough any text by wrapping HTML `<del>` or `<s>` tags around the text.
- Underline text by wrapping it with HTML `<ins>` and `<u>` tags

- You can also use the HTML `<small>` tags inside the paragraph tags to display smaller text relative to other text around the paragraph.
- You can apply the bold feature to text using HTML `<b>` and `<strong>` tags
- Italicize text using HTML `<em>` and `<i>` tags

Aligning text

Bootstrap provides helper classes for alignment of textual content. These classes are:

- `text-left`
- `text-right`
- `text-center`
- `text-justify`
- `text-nowrap`

Let's apply `text-right` to the preceding paragraph text and checkout how it realigns the text:

```
<p class="lead text-right">
    Lorem ipsum dolor sit amet, consectetur adipiscing elit.
        In fringilla dictum libero, vel placerat lorem elementum
            tristique.
</p>
```

The output will look as follows:

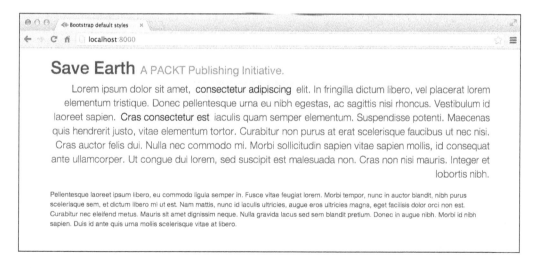

You can see that the text is now aligned to the right with respect to the position of the container.

The `text-nowrap` class removes the automatic line break and lets the paragraph appear in a single line, as shown in following screenshot:

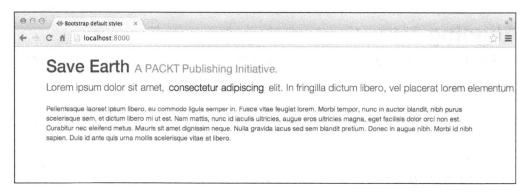

Try playing with other alignment classes and check out the changes in the browser.

Text transformation

Transforming a text to uppercase, lowercase, or capitalizing it are sometimes very necessary actions in some web applications. Bootstrap has got classes to perform these transformations:

- `text-lowercase`
- `text-uppercase`
- `text-capitalize`

Text transformation through CSS or using Bootstrap's classes is definitely not recommended while designing websites. Crawlers and search engines parse the text while it is actually written in a webpage. CSS simply helps in changing the way it is displayed in the browser.

Blockquotes

Blockquotes are very important Bootstrap components. They are used to quote some important information or popular sayings. Let's check out how to create a blockquote in Bootstrap.

Place the following markup inside the container of our static website.

```
<blockquote>
```

```
  <p>Lorem ipsum dolor sit amet, consectetur adipiscing
    elit. Integer posuere erat a ante.</p>
</blockquote>
```

It will produce the following output in the browser:

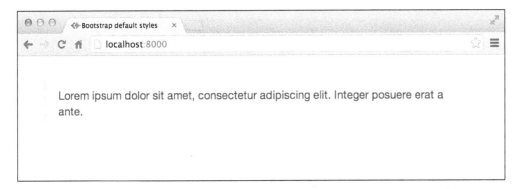

You can see that a vertical bar is placed to the left of `blockquote`. Blockquote comes with many customization options in Bootstrap. For example, placing a `<footer>` element inside the `blockquote` code will be as follows:

```
<blockquote>
  <p>Lorem ipsum dolor sit amet, consectetur adipiscing
    elit. Integer posuere erat a ante.</p>
  <footer>by Syed Fazle Rahman</footer>
</blockquote>
```

The output for the preceding code will look as follows:

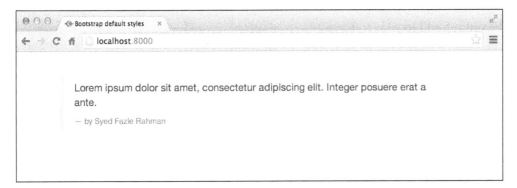

You can also change the alignment of blockquote by applying the class `blockquote-reverse`. It will make the blockquote look as shown in the following screenshot:

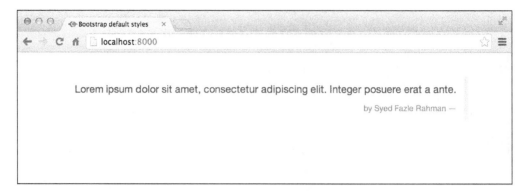

Styling listing elements

List elements, the `<ol>` ordered element, and the `<ul>` unordered element, play a very important role in the web. They are used to create a list of items such as creating menus, listing features, and so on. Bootstrap comes with some default styles for these elements. It resets the browser's default style and adds a minimal style to them. Let's style the listing elements:

```
<ul>
<li>Call Mommy</li>
<li>Go out for dinner tonight</li>
<li>Call Girlfriend(s) ;-)</li>
<li>Attend tomorrow's lecture</li>
</ul>
```

The output will look as follows:

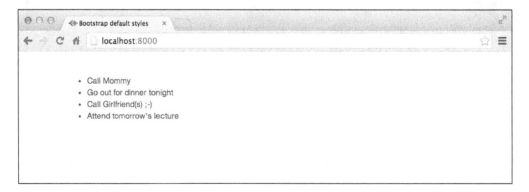

Now, let us look at ordered lists:

```
<ol>
  <li>Call Mommy</li>
  <li>Go out for dinner tonight</li>
  <li>Call Girlfriend(s) ;-)</li>
  <li>Attend tomorrow's lecture</li>
</ol>
```

The output for the preceding code will look as follows:

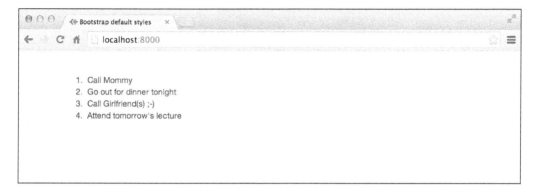

Let's add some helper classes by Bootstrap to modify the look of, lists. Adding the class list-inline to any of the preceding lists will make the list items appear inline, that is, side by side, as shown in the following screenshot:

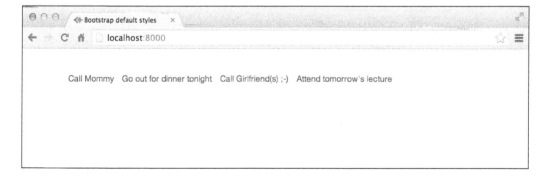

Adding the class `list-unstyled` to any of the list elements will remove the bullets or numbers from the list items. These are shown in the following screenshot:

Let's experiment a bit and nest the unordered list to check out whether Bootstrap still supports us:

```
<ul>
  <li>Call Mommy</li>
  <li>Go out for dinner tonight</li>
  <li>
    Call Girlfriend(s) ;-)
    <ul>
    <li>Julie</li>
    <li>Marry</li>
    <li>Monalisa</li>
    <li>Others :-D</li>
    </ul>
  </li>
  <li>Attend tomorrow's lecture</li>
</ul>
```

The output for the preceding code will look as follows:

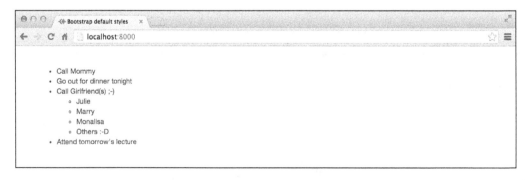

Oh yes! Bootstrap does support the nested list. Try experimenting with another list and a combination of helper classes. To change the style of bullets, you need to write your own style. Take the following code as an example:

```
ul{
list-style-type: circle;
}
```

Creating and styling buttons

In the preceding chapter, we saw a gist of how buttons are created in Bootstrap. Any anchor tag `<a>` or `<button>` tag can be made to look like a fancy button using Bootstrap. To create a button, you need to use the class `.btn` in combination with many other helper button classes. There are two different types of button classes in Bootstrap: for different sizes and for different colors.

The button classes for different colors are as follows:

- `btn-primary`: This button class is used for creating a dark-blue button
- `btn-info`: This is used for creating a light-blue button
- `btn-success`: This button class is used for creating a green-colored button
- `btn-warning`: This class is used for creating a pale yellow-colored button
- `btn-danger`: This is used for creating a red-colored button
- `btn-default`: This class is used for creating a white-colored button
- `btn-link`: This class is used to make buttons look like a link while preserving the behavior of a button

Let's see the buttons in action. Here's the markup for creating a single button:

```
<a href="http://www.packtpub.com/" class="btn btn-success">
  PACKT Pub
</a>
```

The following screenshot shows all the buttons in action:

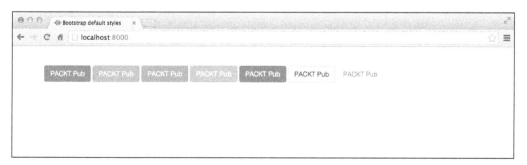

Bootstrap also has classes for creating buttons of various sizes. These classes have to be combined, along with the combination of `btn` and color classes. Classes for various sizes are:

- `btn-lg`: This class is used to create a large button
- `btn-sm`: This class is used to create a small button
- `btn-xs`: This class is used to create an extremely small button
- `No class`: This class is used for a default size button

The following example shows a demo of using these classes:

```
<a href="http://www.packtpub.com/" class="btn btn-primary
  btn-lg">
  PACKT Pub
</a>
```

Here's a screenshot displaying all button sizes:

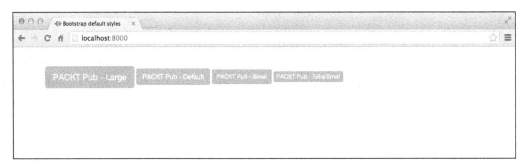

Bootstrap buttons also come with various states like active, disabled, and so on. The attributes of the Bootstrap button are as follows:

- The `active` state: When you click on a Bootstrap button, this state is automatically added to a button. If you want a button to always look like an active button, then add the class `active` to it:

```
<a href="http://www.packtpub.com/" class="btn btn-info
  btn-lg active">
  PACKT Pub - Active
</a>
```

The `active` state of the button can been seen in this screenshot:

As seen in the preceding zoomed image, an active button gets an inset shadow effect.

- The `disabled` state: To make a button disabled, just add a `disabled` attribute to it:

```
<a href="http://www.packtpub.com/" class="btn
  btn-info btn-lg" disabled>
  PACKT Pub - Disabled
</a>
```

A disabled button is not clickable.

In case of a `<button>` tag, you need to provide a disabled value to the `disabled` attribute:

```
<button type="button" class="btn btn-lg btn-primary"
  disabled="disabled">
  PACKT Pub - Disabled
</button>
```

Which elements are eligible to use Bootstrap's button classes?

This is one of the most important things to remember. You cannot apply button classes to any HTML element. There are only four different types of elements that can be used as Bootstrap's button:

- The HTML anchor tag: `<a>`
- The HTML button tag: `<button>`
- The HTML input tag with button type: `<input type="button" />`
- The HTML input tag with submit type: `<input type="submit" />`

Styling images in Bootstrap

Images are essential to any web application. It is very important to display them properly. Bootstrap comes with many different classes that will help you to display images appropriately in your web app.

When we talk about responsive images, we mean an image that fits to the size of its container irrespective of its own size. Creating a responsive image in Bootstrap is just a matter of a single class. This feature is especially useful when you are creating a portal for users, and you aren't aware of the size of image they are going to upload. Hence, adding Bootstrap's responsive class to it will be very helpful in such scenarios. You should also remember that Bootstrap won't change the size of the actual image. It will just resize it using CSS properties.

The class used for creating a responsive image is `img-responsive`. Let's create a grid using Bootstrap's grid system and then add a responsive image to checkout how it fits to the size of the grid. The steps to add a responsive image are:

```
<div class="container">
  <div class="row">
    <div class="col-xs-4" style="background: grey">
      <img src="packt_logo.png" class="img-responsive">
    </div>
  </div>
</div>
```

The output of the preceding code will look as follows:

I have used the background color to display the range of the grid. You can see that the image fits to the grid.

Bootstrap also offers some helper classes for decorating the image on the go. The helper classes of Bootstrap are:

- `img-rounded`: This creates a square image but with slightly rounded corners.
- `img-circle`: This produces a circular image.
- `img-thumbnail`: This gives the image a clickable effect. This also adds a hover effect on the image.

The following screenshot shows all the preceding classes, respectively:

In our `Online Packt Shopping` application, we have used the responsive image class to display the product listing on the homepage.

Summary

Hope you enjoyed using various styling classes of Bootstrap. You can head over to Bootstrap's online documentation (`http://getbootstrap.com/css/`) to know about more CSS classes. We will be using these Bootstrap classes very frequently in the upcoming chapters, where we will focus on completing our shopping application.

5
Reinventing Tables and Forms in Bootstrap

Tables and forms are good old fashioned features of HTML. They have been playing a pivotal role on the Internet since its inception. With Bootstrap and Rails, we are going to reinvent a whole new way of creating forms and tables in our web applications.

In this chapter, we will take a look at various features of Bootstrap tables and forms. We will use Bootstrap's validation classes while validating forms in a Rails app. Finally, we will use Bootstrap's tables to fill the stored data.

We will continue to develop the same demo application that was half designed in the last chapter. We will now see how to modify the single-product page by using Bootstrap's tables. There are some more pages which were left unstyled in the last chapter: the New Product Form page and Edit Product Form page. We will use Bootstrap forms to modify these pages as well.

However, before jumping into the application, we need to understand how Bootstrap's tables and forms are created. Hence, we will start by creating dummy products, as always, and then integrate them in our real application.

Creating Bootstrap tables

Bootstrap tables are normal HTML tables, along with some special classes provided by Bootstrap. These classes come with various different CSS styles to be applied to the HTML tables. Hence, Bootstrap gives you multiple classes to create different types of tables, as per your requirements.

So, let's create a basic HTML table first. For this, create a dummy project called `Bootstrap Tables` and create an `index.html` file. Copy the following Bootstrap recommended HTML markup into this file:

```
<!DOCTYPE html>
<html lang="en">
  <head>
    <meta charset="utf-8">
    <meta http-equiv="X-UA-Compatible" content="IE=edge">
    <meta name="viewport" content="width=device-width,
      initial-scale=1">
    <title>Bootstrap Tables</title>
    <!-- Bootstrap -->
    <link rel="stylesheet" href="http://maxcdn.bootstrapcdn.com/
      bootstrap/3.2.0/css/bootstrap.min.css">
  </head>
  <body>
    <!-- jQuery (necessary for Bootstrap's JavaScript plugins) -->
    <script src="https://ajax.googleapis.com/ajax/libs/jquery/
      1.11.1/jquery.min.js"></script>
    <!-- Include all compiled plugins (below), or include
      individual files as needed -->
    <script src="http://maxcdn.bootstrapcdn.com/bootstrap/
      3.2.0/js/bootstrap.min.js"></script>
  </body>
</html>
```

This file has all the necessary Bootstrap files included from the CDN. Let's proceed with Bootstrap container and insert code into the file:

```
<div class="container">
</div>
```

Let's create an HTML table inside this container:

```
<div class="container">
  <table>
    <tr>
      <th>Item Name</th>
      <th>Price ($)</th>
    </tr>
    <tr>
      <td>Item 1</td>
      <td>$114</td>
    </tr>
    <tr>
      <td>Item 2</td>
      <td>$234</td>
```

```
    </tr>
  </table>
</div>
```

If you preview the preceding markup in the browser, you will see a *not-so-awesome* table with two columns, here's the screenshot:

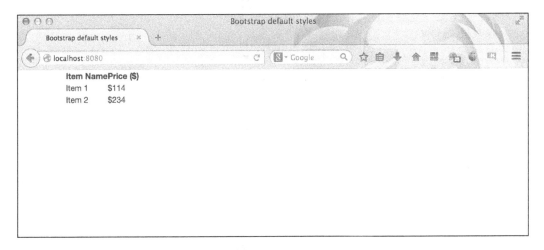

It's time to check out the magic of Bootstrap. Just add the `table` class to the preceding table in the screenshot, and you will find a properly aligned and decent table:

```
<div class="container">
  <table class="table">
  </table>
</div>
```

After inserting the preceding code, you'll get something like the following screenshot:

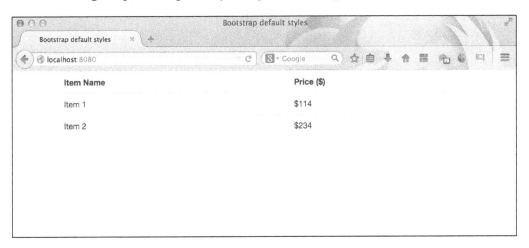

That's great, isn't it?

Let's explore more. Now, add a .table-striped class to the preceding table in the screenshot. Also, keep the .table class in the table markup. Here, .table-striped is a helper class to add an additional alternate striped style to the table:

```
<div class="container">
  <table class="table table-striped">
  </table>
</div>
```

You should get something like the following screenshot:

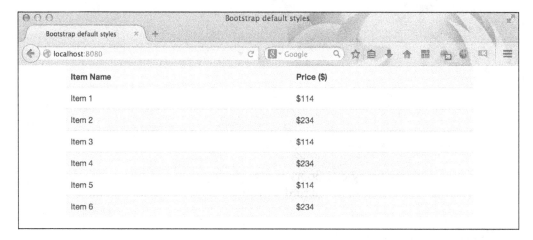

There's more. To get a bordered table, this time add the .table-bordered class to the table class:

```
<div class="container">
  <table class="table table-bordered">
  </table>
</div>
```

The output will be as follows:

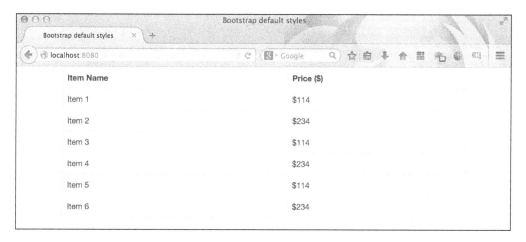

Some other helper classes include:

- .table-hover: Adding this class to the table highlights a row when the mouse is hovered over it.
- .table-condensed: Add this class when you want to reduce the amount of spacing in each cell.

You should not restrict yourself to combining the preceding classes together in a single table. I leave this up to you to experiment.

There are five different contextual classes in Bootstrap. These classes are added to a particular row to highlight them with a particular color. The five contextual classes in Bootstrap are:

- active: This is added for a light grey background color
- success: This is added for a light green background color
- danger: This is added for a reddish brown background color
- info: This is added for a light blue background color
- warning: This is added for a light yellow background color

The following screenshot shows all the preceding contextual classes in action:

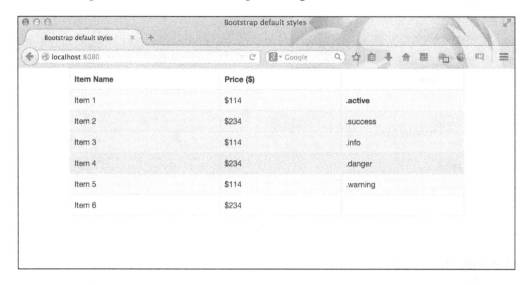

The preceding contextual class can also be applied to a particular cell. For example:

```
<tr>
  <td class="warning">Warning text here</td>
</tr>
```

This will only highlight that cell, instead of the whole row.

Let's talk about the responsiveness of the Bootstrap table. By default, Bootstrap tables are responsive in nature. They change their overall width and also the width of the columns, as per the size of the browser window. There might be times when you have hundreds of columns in your table, and you need to view it in a mobile screen. Imagine 100 columns dividing the table width into 100 equal parts. Too untidy, isn't it?

Well, here's Bootstrap to the rescue! Bootstrap gives you a class called `.table-responsive`, which adds a horizontal scroll bar to the table when the space isn't sufficient. This also makes the table responsive to the touch-based scrolls in mobile screens.

Please note that you shouldn't use these tables to structure the web pages. A table-based layout is outdated and is generally considered bad from an SEO point of view. You should only use tables to display tabular data.

Creating Bootstrap forms

Creating forms in Bootstrap is as easy as creating tables, which we have just seen in the previous section. All you need is some HTML markup and proper Bootstrap classes for forms. In this section, we will again create a dummy project called `Bootstrap Forms` and add an `index.html` file. Also, fill this file with the basic Bootstrap recommended HTML, as shown in the previous section. Do not forget to add the Bootstrap container in it.

Let's add a simple `<form>` tag to the preceding container:

```
<div class="container">
  <form>
  </form>
</div>
```

You don't have to attach any class to the form tag. The classes here are added to the form elements.

Let's add our first form element to our form. We will place a text field and an associated label element. Bootstrap allows you to create a form group which consists of a label and a text field. This helps Bootstrap to properly style the form elements. A form group is created using a `div` element with a `.form-group` class. Let's add a form group to the preceding form:

```
<div class="container">
  <form>
    <div class="form-group">
      <label for="emailField">Email address</label>
      <input type="text" class="form-control" id="emailField"
        placeholder="Enter email">
    </div>
  </form>
</div>
```

We have also added a `.form-control` class to the text field to apply Bootstrap's style for text-based fields. You can also add this class to other text-based fields such as `<textarea>`, `<datetime>`, `<email>`, and so on.

The preceding form should now look as shown in the following screenshot:

In a similar way, we will fill the preceding form with a **password** field:

```
<div class="form-group">
  <label for="passwordField">Password</label>
  <input type="password" class="form-control"
    id="passwordField" placeholder="Enter email">
</div>
```

This gives us the form represented in the following screenshot:

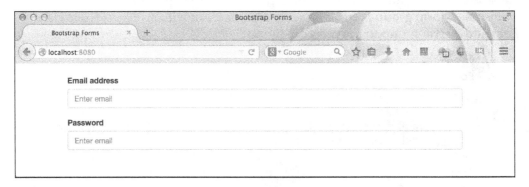

It's time to add a `checkbox` and a `radio` button to the form. Bootstrap provides a different set of classes for checkbox and radio buttons, `.form-control` isn't compatible with them. This time, we will create wrappers with `checkbox` and `radio` classes. For example:

```
<div class="checkbox">
  <label>
```

```
    <input type="checkbox"> Remember me
  </label>
</div>
```

This will create a properly aligned checkbox to your form. Just replace `checkbox` with `.radio` and create a `radio` button inside it:

```
<div class="radio">
  <label>
    <input type="radio"> Male
  </label>
</div>
<div class="radio">
  <label>
    <input type="radio"> Female
  </label>
</div>
```

For now, we will go with the checkbox element in our form, as shown here:

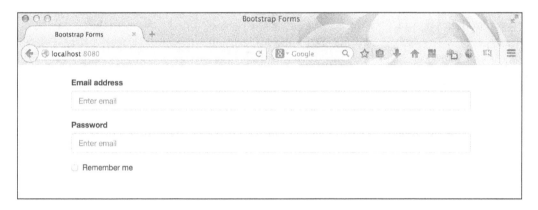

Finally, let's add a `submit` button to the form. The markup for a submit button is as follows:

```
<button type="submit" class="btn btn-success">Sign in</button>
```

This is a basic Bootstrap button with `btn` and `.btn-success` classes. The first class gives it the shape of a button, while the second class applies a color to it.

Our final Bootstrap form will now look like the following screenshot:

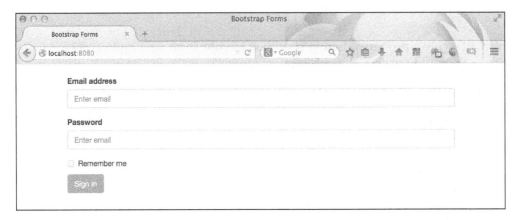

You can also create different types of forms in Bootstrap. For example, if you want to place a login form inside the top-thin navigation bar of your website then the preceding form is definitely not suited for it.

Bootstrap lets you place all the form elements in line or side by side, so that it can be fitted properly in such situations. To create an inline form, you just need a single class, as always, `.form-inline`. You need to add this class to the preceding `<form>` tag.

```
<form class="form-inline">
  ...
</form>
```

You should get the following output:

I know you are surprised here! Bootstrap added a single line of CSS code to `.form-group` when the `.form-inline` class was added. Here's the code snapshot from Bootstrap's CSS:

```
.form-inline .form-group{
  display: inline-block;
}
```

There is another very useful HTML form element called `<select>` used to create a drop-down menu. You can add the `.form-control` class to remove the default browser style from it and apply Bootstrap's style. For example:

```
<select class="form-control">
  <option>1</option>
  <option>2</option>
  <option>3</option>
  <option>4</option>
  <option>5</option>
</select>
```

To disable a field in a Bootstrap form, just add HTML5's disabled attribute to any text field. Bootstrap will apply a deactivated style to it. This is applicable to `text-based` fields, `checkboxes`, `radio buttons`, `form buttons`, and the `<select>` element.

You can also control the sizes of each text-based field and select elements in Bootstrap using the following sizing classes:

- `.input-lg`: Adding `.input-lg` to a text field will make it look bigger than the default style

- `.input-sm`: Adding `.input-sm` to a text field will make it look smaller than the default style

Sometimes, you might need to add a `help` text below each form field. To do this, you need to add a `span` element with the `.help-block` class inside the `.form-group` element. For example:

```
<div class="form-group">
  <label class="control-label" for="emailField">
    Email Address</label>
    <input type="text" class="form-control" id="emailField">
    <span class="help-block">Enter a valid email address.
    </span>
  </span>
</div>
```

Validation classes in Bootstrap forms

Bootstrap works well with HTML5's default form validation. Adding an attribute called required to any form element will prevent the form from being submitted. Bootstrap's JavaScript doesn't have any predefined validation functionality. It provides you with CSS classes that can be applied to the form elements on runtime. These classes are important to highlight which form element needs attention by the user.

Let's have a look at some of the form validation classes by Bootstrap:

- `.has-error`: This class is used to highlight a red color
- `.has-warning`: This class is used to highlight a dull yellow color
- `.has-success`: This class is used to highlight a green color

These classes are applied to the `.form-group` element. For example, adding the `.has-error` class to any `.form-group` element will highlight both label and form elements with a red color:

```
<div class="form-group has-error">
  <label for="emailField">Email address</label>
  <input type="text" class="form-control" id="emailField"
    placeholder="Enter email">
</div>
```

You should get something like the following:

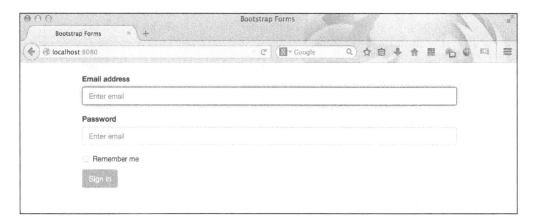

Please note that Bootstrap will not add the validation classes automatically. You have to programmatically add them to highlight the errors.

You can also display fancy validation icons beside each form element. For this, you need to add a `.has-feedback` class to the `.form-group` element. You also have to add a span element with a Glyphicon icon in it. For example:

```
<div class="form-group has-success has-feedback">
  <label class="control-label" for="textField">
    Input with success</label>
  <input type="text" class="form-control" id="textField">
  <span class="glyphicon glyphicon-ok
    form-control-feedback"></span>
</div>
```

The preceding code will give you the following output:

Adding Bootstrap tables to our Rails application

In our application, **OnlinePacktShopping**, we have a `product details` page. We will be adding Bootstrap's table to this page and do the redesigning.

Start the server and check out the product page, it should look like this:

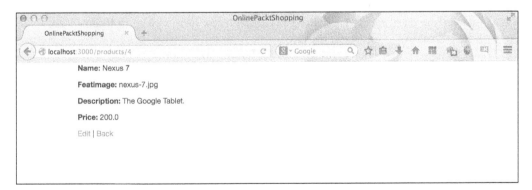

We are going to redesign the page using Bootstrap, it should look like this:

The product page is displayed using the `show.html.erb` view present in the `products` folder. To reach this folder, navigate to `app/views/products/`. Open this page and delete the entire markup from it.

First, we need to carry the page header style from the home page to this screen. So, put the following markup in the file:

```
<div class="page-header">
  <h3></h3>
</div>
```

In the home page, we used to display **All products** using the `<h3>` tag. This time we will fill it with the name of the product. The product name is carried to this view by the `@product` model using the `name` property. Hence, `@product.name` should give us the name of the product:

```
<div class="page-header">
  <h3><%= @product.name %></h3>
</div>
```

Next, we want to place two default action buttons, **Edit** and **Back**, on this page header. We have to place both these buttons side by side. Hence, we will use Bootstrap's `list-inline` component here:

```
<div class="page-header">
  <ul class="list-inline">
    <li><%= link_to 'Edit', edit_product_path(@product),
      :class=>"btn btn-warning" %></li>
    <li><%= link_to 'Back', products_path, :class=>"btn
      btn-default" %></li>
  </ul>
  <h3><%= @product.name %></h3>
</div>
```

As you can see in the preceding screenshot, I have used `link_to` tag to create links dynamically. The path is produced using the `edit_product_path()` and `products_path` methods. I am also adding classes `.btn`, `.btn-warning` and `.btn-default` to the buttons. This will produce a screen that looks like the following:

I have used `.btn-warning` just to achieve the orange-colored button. It is not related to any warning sign here.

Let's pull those buttons to the right side using Bootstrap's helper class `.pull-right` added to the `<ul>` tag:

Now, we have our buttons placed properly. Let's create a Bootstrap table to display product data in it:

```
<table class="table table-bordered">
</table>
```

I am using a bordered table here. Let's proceed to create rows and columns:

```
<table class="table table-bordered">
  <tr>
    <td>Name</td>
    <td><%= @product.name %></td>
  </tr>
  <tr>
    <td>Image</td>
    <td><img class="img-responsive" src=<%=asset_path
      @product.featImage %>/></td>
  </tr>
  <tr>
    <td>Description</td>
    <td><%= @product.description %></td>
  </tr>
  <tr class="success">
    <td>Price</td>
    <td><%= @product.price %></td>
  </tr>
</table>
```

As you can see in the preceding code, I have displayed all the data present inside @ product model in each row. I have also highlighted the last row using the . success class. The preceding markup will give us a page that looks like the following:

That was easy! Wasn't it?

We still have to show the notice object when it is passed from the Edit page and Create page to product page. Since this message is not always visible, we will use a conditional if statement to display it in this product page.

Go ahead and add the following markup above the table:

```
<% if notice %>
  <div class="alert alert-info">
    <p id="notice"><%= notice %></p>
  </div>
<% end %>
```

I am using Bootstrap's alert feature here using the `alert` and `.alert-info` class. The first class is used to space and properly align the text and the second class is used for giving a proper background color. We will discuss more on alerts in the upcoming sections. The preceding markup will look like the following:

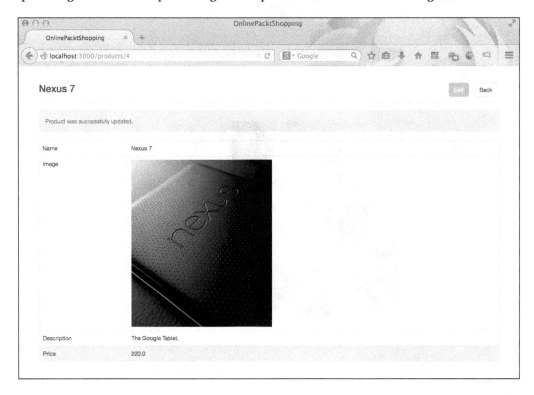

Finally, we are done with the product display page. We will now proceed to design the `Add product` and `Edit product` views.

Adding Bootstrap forms to our Rails application

There are two template files that we have to edit here: `new.html.erb` and `edit.html.erb`. Open and view them. You will find that both of these files have the exact same structure. There's only one additional **Show product** button in the `edit.html.erb` template. Hence, we will design only one form, `new.html.erb`, and then reuse it in the second template.

First, delete everything that's inside `new.html.erb`. As we did in all the pages, we will create a `page-header` in this page too. To do this, add the following markup:

```
<div class="page-header">
  <h3>Add new product</h3>
</div>
```

Let's proceed to add a **cancel** button to the home page in the preceding `page-header`:

```
<div class="page-header">
  <%= link_to 'Cancel', products_path, :class=>"btn
    btn-default pull-right" %>
  <h3>Add new product</h3>
</div>
```

Since we are having only button, we don't have to use Bootstrap's `list-inline` feature here, as shown in the following screenshot:

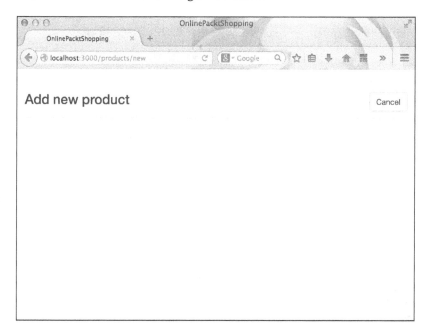

It's time to create a form for creating new products. We will use Bootstrap's grid system to create an 8-Bootstrap-columns container form. The markup for this is as follows:

```
<div class="row">
  <div class="col-xs-8 col-xs-offset-2">
  </div>
</div>
```

We have used an offset class to center align the whole container. Next, we will add the tag to render the form inside the preceding container:

```
<div class="row">
  <div class="col-xs-8 col-xs-offset-2">
    <%= render 'form' %>
  </div>
</div>
```

The preceding code will fetch the old unstyled form from the `_form.html.erb` template. So, let's style the form present in this template. Here's the modified markup:

```
<%= form_for(@product) do |f| %>
  <% if @product.errors.any? %>
  <div id="error_explanation">
    <h2><%= pluralize(@product.errors.count, "error") %>
      prohibited this product from being saved:</h2>
    <ul>
  <% @product.errors.full_messages.each do |message| %>
  <li><%= message %></li>
  <% end %>
  </ul>
  </div>
  <% end %>
  <div class="form-group">
    <%= f.label :name, :for=>"nameField" %><br>
    <%= f.text_field :name, :class=>"form-control",
      :id=>"nameField" %>
  </div>
  <div class="form-group">
    <%= f.label :featImage, :for=>"imgField" %><br>
    <%= f.text_field :featImage, :class=>"form-control",
      :id=>"imgField" %>
  </div>
  <div class="form-group">
    <%= f.label :description,:for=>"descField" %><br>
    <%= f.text_area :description, :class=>"form-control",
      :id=>"descField" %>
  </div>
  <div class="form-group">
    <%= f.label :price, :for=>"priceField" %><br>
    <%= f.text_field :price, :class=>"form-control",
      :id=>"priceField" %>
```

```
    </div>
    <ul class="list-inline">
      <li><%= f.submit 'Create', :class=>"btn btn-success" %></li>
      <li><%= button_tag "Reset", type: :reset, :class=>
        "btn btn-default" %></li>
    </ul>
  <% end %>
```

If you look carefully, you'll see that, I have wrapped all the labels and their respective form elements inside a .form-group element. For each label, I have added a for attribute with the value as the ID of its corresponding form element. For each text field, I have added a class as .form-control and an ID attribute with a unique ID value.

At the end, I have used Bootstrap's list-inline feature to align two action buttons: **Submit** and **Reset**. I have added class btn-success to the submit button and btn-default to the reset button.

It's time to checkout the whole Add product page in the browser. If you have implemented everything correctly, you should get a screen that looks like the following:

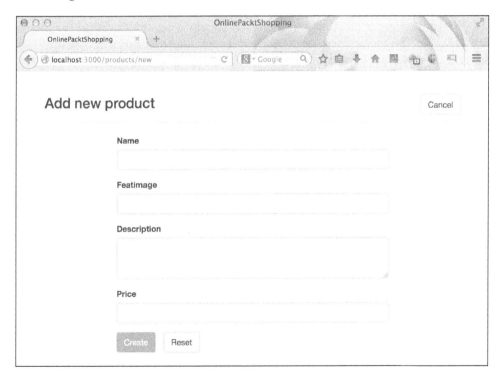

We will now move on to edit the edit.html.erb template file. We just need to make some modifications to the new.html.erb file's markup to make it ready for edit. html.erb. Copy all the contents of the new.html.erb file and paste it in the edit. html.erb file. Change the text in the page-header to Edit Product. We need to add an additional button to this section, the Show Product Button. Hence, the final markup for the page-header in this file is as follows:

```
<div class="page-header">
  <ul class="list-inline pull-right">
    <li><%= link_to 'Show Product', @product, :class=>
      "btn btn-success" %></li>
    <li><%= link_to 'Cancel', products_path, :class=>"btn btn-
      default" %></li>
  </ul>
  <h3>Add new product</h3>
</div>
```

Summary

In this chapter, we saw how to create dummy Bootstrap forms and tables. We saw many different types of variations in them which could be done by simply changing or replacing Bootstrap classes. We then moved on to learn various Bootstrap validation classes for forms.

We saw how to use helper classes to make both forms and tables even more exciting. Finally, we moved on to integrate both Bootstrap forms and tables in our application, OnlinePacktShopping. We also completed the whole design of our basic application using Bootstrap's features. In the upcoming chapter, we will learn about Bootstrap navigation bars.

6
Creating Navigation Bars

Creating a navigation bar has been one of the most difficult tasks for a novice web designer or a web developer, with no experience in web designing. One has to take care of properly aligning links, overflows, styling links, making the whole bar responsive, and so on.

Bootstrap gives you plenty of choice to create and design a navigation bar without diving deep into its CSS. Just like creating any other components in Bootstrap, creating a navigation bar also requires us to follow a proper markup structure. In this article, we will learn how to create a Bootstrap navigation bar, and how we can modify it to fit our needs. We will also check out various other ways of representing a navigation bar in a website. We will also integrate a fixed navigation bar in our current application, OnlinePacktShopping.

Getting started with a navigation bar

As always, we will start by creating a dummy project to learn and create a static navigation bar. Create a folder called BootstrapNavigation and create an index. html file in it. We will use the same Bootstrap recommended HTML markup for the navigation bar, the code is as follows:

```
<!DOCTYPE html>
<html lang="en">
  <head>
    <meta charset="utf-8">
    <meta http-equiv="X-UA-Compatible" content="IE=edge">
    <meta name="viewport" content="width=device-width,
      initial-scale=1">
    <title>Bootstrap Navigation Bar</title>
    <!-- Bootstrap -->
    <link rel="stylesheet" href="http://maxcdn.bootstrapcdn.com/
      bootstrap/3.2.0/css/bootstrap.min.css">
```

```
    </head>
    <body>
      <h1>Hello World</h1>
      <!-- jQuery (necessary for Bootstrap's JavaScript plugins) -->
      <script src="https://ajax.googleapis.com/ajax/
        libs/jquery/1.11.1/jquery.min.js"></script>
      <!-- Include all compiled plugins (below), or include
        individual files as needed -->
      <script src="http://maxcdn.bootstrapcdn.com/bootstrap/
        3.2.0/js/bootstrap.min.js"></script>
    </body>
</html>
```

As per the preceding code, a some point, you should have a **Hello World** message on your browser window. Let's proceed and remove this message. To create a navigation bar, we need to create a `div` class with the `navbar` attribute:

```
<div class="navbar">
</div>
```

Then, we need to select a color for the navigation bar we want to use. Bootstrap gives you two different color variants: default gray and inverted black. They can be applied by using the `.navbar-default` and `.navbar-inverted` classes, respectively. We will proceed with `.navbar-default` in our application:

```
<div class="navbar navbar-default">

</div>
```

Next, we have added a container to wrap all the elements of the navigation bar and set the proper overflow. We will use `.container-fluid` to create a full-width container instead of a fixed one. This will allow us to use all the available space inside the `.navbar` element. The code is as follows:

```
<div class="navbar navbar-default">

  <div class="container-fluid">

  </div>

</div>
```

You can use the `.container` class for a fixed width container inside the navigation bar. The navbar is divided into two important sections:

- `.navbar-header`: This is used for inserting a website's branding

- `.navbar-collapse`: This is used to collect all the links and other useful stuff that go inside a navigation bar

So, let's proceed and create each one of them step by step. Insert `.navbar-header` in our markup:

```
<div class="navbar navbar-default">
  <div class="container-fluid">
    <div class="navbar-header">
    </div>
  </div>
</div>
```

We will now place the website's name/branding using the `anchor` tag. Remember to add a `.navbar-brand` class to apply an appropriate style to `index.html`. Let's try adding more elements into it:

```
<div class="navbar navbar-default">
  <div class="container-fluid">
    <div class="navbar-header">
      <a href="#">OnlinePacktShopping</a>
    </div>
  </div>
</div>
```

If you check out the `index.html` file now, you should see something like this:

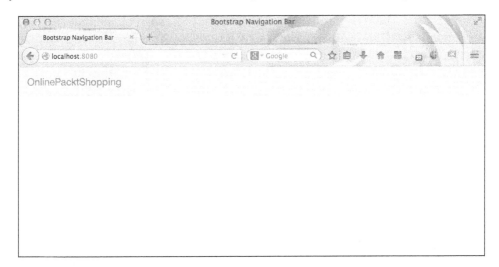

Next, we will see one of the most important elements of the navigation bar, the collapsed icon. This icon is visible when the website is opened in small browsers, such as cell phones. This icon will then be responsible for opening the collapsed menu when tapped on. Let's try adding .navbar-collapse element:

```
<div class="navbar-header">
  <button type="button" class="navbar-toggle collapsed"
    data-toggle="collapse" data-target="#collapsibleMenu">
  <span class="icon-bar"></span>
  <span class="icon-bar"></span>
  <span class="icon-bar"></span>
  </button>
  <a href="#" class="navbar-brand">OnlinePacktShopping</a>
</div>
```

As you can see in the preceding code, this button should be placed inside the
`.navbar-header` class. It should have a `.navbar-toggle collapsed` class. The
first class here, is used to apply proper styling and pull it to the right side of the
navigation bar. The second class is used to keep a track of the state of the button
from collapsed to noncollapsed. You should also add two custom-data attributes
to this element: `data-toggle` and `data-target`. The first one is used to initiate
the collapse functionality in Bootstrap's JavaScript and the second attribute is used
to identify the target menu to add the collapse functionality. The `data-target`
attribute should contain the ID of the menu, which will be collapsing on smaller
browsers. We will create this menu soon.

Inside this button, there should be three different HTML span elements.
These elements have an `icon-bar` class, which is responsible for drawing small,
horizontal lines. So, when all three of them are placed together, we get a stacked-like
icon. If you resize the browser window to a smaller size, you will find this button
placed to the right of the navigation bar. Let's see the output:

We are done with `navbar-header` here. Let's proceed to the `.navbar-collapse` element. This element will wrap all the navigation bar links, search fields, dropdowns, and so on. Make sure that you add this element as a sibling to `.navbar-header` and not inside .navbar- header. Let's add the collapse element into it:.

```
<div class="collapse navbar-collapse" id="collapibleMenu">
</div>
```

This element should contain the same ID as used in the data-target attribute of the `.navbar-toggle` button. When you click on the **toggle** button, this whole portion will be toggled. Next, we will add some links to our navigation bar. We will use an unordered list with `nav` and `.navbar-nav` classes added to it. Both these classes are for styling purposes.

```
<ul class="nav navbar-nav">
</ul>
```

Insert links using the `<li>` tag and the `<a>` tag, as follows:

```
<ul class="nav navbar-nav">
  <li><a href="#">Home</a></li>
  <li><a href="#">About us</a></li>
  <li><a href="#">Contact us</a></li>
  <li><a href="#">Support</a></li>
</ul>
```

This should give you a beautiful navigation bar with some links in it, as shown in the following screenshot:

If you try to make the browser window smaller and click on the **toggle** button, you should see a responsive menu in action, as shown in the following screenshot:

Adding the `.navbar-left` and `.navbar-right` classes to the `.navbar-nav` list will align the links to the left and right side of the navigation bar, respectively, as shown in the following screenshot:

As learned in the previous chapter, you can also create a Bootstrap form and place it in the navigation bar. You don't have to add `form-inline` to place form elements horizontally here. Bootstrap gives you a special form class for the navigation bar, `.navbar-form`. Adding this class properly styles the form, as per the navigation bar alignment.

```
<form class="navbar-form navbar-left">
  <div class="form-group">
  <input type="text" class="form-control" placeholder="Search">
  </div>
  <button type="submit" class="btn btn-default">Submit</button>
</form>
```

Make sure that you add the form inside `.navbar-collapse` since it is the wrapper of all the navigation bar elements. This should give you a navigation bar, as shown in the following screenshot:

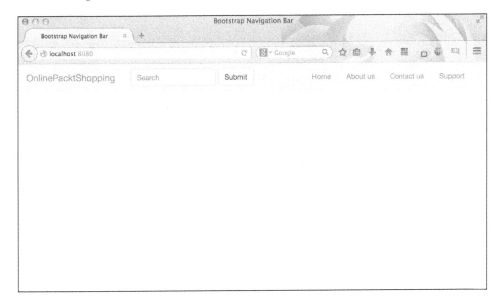

The final markup for the navigation bar, till now, is as follows:

```
<div class="navbar navbar-default">
  <div class="container-fluid">
    <div class="navbar-header">
      <button type="button" class="navbar-toggle collapsed"
        data-toggle="collapse" data-target="#collapibleMenu">
        <span class="icon-bar"></span>
        <span class="icon-bar"></span>
        <span class="icon-bar"></span>
```

```
      </button>
      <a href="#" class="navbar-brand">OnlinePacktShopping</a>
    </div>
    <div class="collapse navbar-collapse" id="collapibleMenu">
      <ul class="nav navbar-nav navbar-right">
      <li><a href="#">Home</a></li>
      <li><a href="#">About us</a></li>
      <li><a href="#">Contact us</a></li>
      <li><a href="#">Support</a></li>
      </ul>
      <form class="navbar-form navbar-left" role="search">
        <div class="form-group">
        <input type="text" class="form-control"
          placeholder="Search">
        </div>
        <button type="submit" class="btn btn-
          default">Submit</button>
      </form>
    </div>
  </div>
</div>
```

Navigation bar helper classes

There are many helper classes available for navigation bar elements. Some of them are as follows:

- .navbar-btn: When you want to place a Bootstrap button in a navigation bar, use this class to properly align it

- .navbar-text: If you want to display some plain text, use this class to make it properly visible

- .navbar-link: If you want to add a link, but not inside the .nav element, then use this class

- .navbar-fixed-top: If you add this class to the parent of the navigation bar navbar, it will stick to the top of the browser window while scrolling

- .navbar-fixed-bottom: This class fixes the navigation bar to the bottom of the window screen and it remains there while scrolling

- .active: Adding this class to any of the <li> elements will highlight the link, as compared to other links

Adding a navigation bar to the Rails application

We will add the preceding navigation bar to our application. We will place our shop's branding in it and also place some links to our company pages. We will also use a black color navigation bar here and make it stick to the top of the browser window.

Go to **App** | **Views** | **Layout** and open the `application.html.erb` file. We will place the navigation bar here, since this will be globally visible throughout the website. Place the following markup above the `.container` element in this file:

```
<div class="navbar navbar-inverted navbar-fixed-top">
  <div class="container-fluid">
    <div class="navbar-header">
      <button type="button" class="navbar-toggle collapsed"
        data-toggle="collapse" data-target="#collapibleMenu">
        <span class="icon-bar"></span>
        <span class="icon-bar"></span>
        <span class="icon-bar"></span>
      </button>
      <a href="#" class="navbar-brand">OnlinePacktShopping</a>
    </div>
    <div class="collapse navbar-collapse"
      id="collapibleMenu">
    <ul class="nav navbar-nav navbar-right">
    <li><a href="#">Home</a></li>
    <li><a href="#">About us</a></li>
    <li><a href="#">Contact us</a></li>
    <li><a href="#">Support</a></li>
    </ul>
    <form class="navbar-form navbar-left" role="search">
    <div class="form-group">
    <input type="text" class="form-control"
      placeholder="Search">
    </div>
    <button type="submit" class="btn btn-
      default">Submit</button>
    </form>
  </div>
  </div>
</div>
```

The website should now look as shown in the following screenshot:

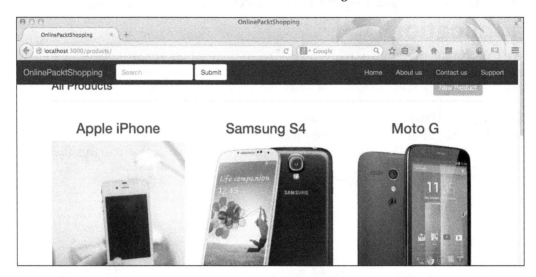

As you can see, there is some overlap here. This is happening because of the `navbar-fixed-top` class. Since the navigation bar is now floating on top of the window, the rest of the body has started to appear from the top of the window as well. We need to write our own small piece of CSS code to fix this situation.

We need to add an additional custom class to the `.container` element in the `application.html.erb` page. Let's give it a `.bodyContent` class:

```
<div class="container bodyContent">
  <%= yield %>
</div>
```

Now, open the `application.css` file by navigating to the **App | Assets | Stylesheets** folder. Add the following CSS code to it:

```
.bodyContent {
  margin-top: 50px;
}
```

We are adding a margin of 50px to the .bodyContent element to push it down as the navigation bar overlaps it. You have a page that now appears properly, as shown in the following screenshot:

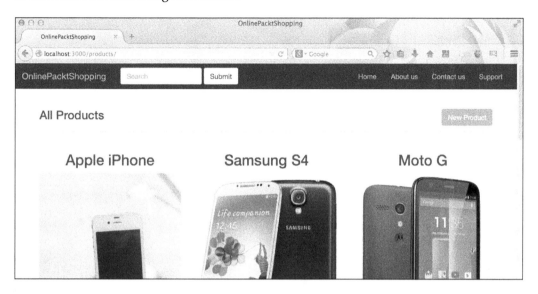

Summary

In this chapter, we saw how to create a simple navigation bar, and how to make it responsive. We also saw how to change the look of the navigation bar by using the .navbar-inverse class. Finally, we went ahead and integrated this navigation bar into our application. I hope you had fun creating a responsive Bootstrap navigation bar.

In the next chapter, we are going to learn about some more Bootstrap components such as breadcrumbs, badges and labels, alerts, and so on. We will also use many of them in our current application.

7
Various Other Bootstrap Components

Until now, we have used some of the most popular Bootstrap components such as forms, buttons, navigation bar, and so on. In this chapter, we will explore some more Bootstrap components, which come ready to use out of the box. We might not be able to use all these components in our existing application, but we will make sure that we don't miss any important ones.

Bootstrap Breadcrumbs

If you are a webmaster, then you must know that Google considers breadcrumbs for the proper SEO of a website. Breadcrumbs are also important for displaying the current page's position, as compared to the whole website. Let's consider that you are viewing a product page on a website. Then, the position of a product might be **Home | Apparels | Jeans | Bare jeans**. This is an example of a breadcrumb. Google and other search engines use breadcrumbs to properly understand a website's hierarchy and the organization of its sub pages.

You can easily create stylish breadcrumbs for your website with Bootstrap. Bootstrap uses traditional HTML ordered list elements to create a breadcrumb. Here's an example of elements:

```
<ol class="breadcrumb">
  <li><a href="#">Home</a></li>
  <li><a href="#">Apparels</a></li>
  <li><a href="#">Jeans</a></li>
  <li class="active">Bare Jeans</li>
</ol>
```

The preceding code creates an elements as shown in the following screenshot:

You can also use HTML's unordered list element in the same style, as in the preceding code. It will give the same result.

The pagination component

You might have seen paginations at the bottom of any blog type website. It will either show previous and next, or page numbers. Pagination helps visitors to easily navigate and skip some content of your website. It also comes in handy while creating a comments section with lots of comments to display.

Bootstrap paginations are also created using HTML's unordered list element You have to use the .pagination class this time:

```
<ul class="pagination">
  <li><a href="#">&laquo;</a></li>
  <li><a href="#">1</a></li>
  <li><a href="#">2</a></li>
  <li><a href="#">3</a></li>
  <li><a href="#" class="active">4</a></li>
  <li><a href="#">5</a></li>
  <li><a href="#">6</a></li>
  <li><a href="#">7</a></li>
  <li><a href="#">&raquo;</a></li>
</ul>
```

In the preceding code, « and » are used to display double angle symbols. This produces the following in the browser:

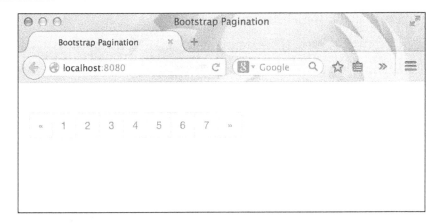

This component also comes with many helper classes such as:

- `.disabled`: This is to make an item in the pagination list non clickable
- `.active`: This is to display the current position of the page
- `.pagination-lg` : This is used for larger pagination buttons
- `.pagination-sm`: This is used for smaller pagination buttons

Bootstrap labels and badges

Labels and badges are very basic components in Bootstrap. You can use them with any text-like components to display a highlighted text. Here's an example of labels and badges:

```
<h3>Packt Publishing <span class="label label-default">New Books!</
span></h3>
```

Labels are created using inline elements such as `<span>`, it has got a class `.label` and many color classes such as `.label-default` for a dark gray color.

Different colors available for labels are:

- `.label-primary`: This is for a dark blue color
- `.label-info`: This is for a light blue color
- `.label-success`: This is for a green color
- `.label-warning`: This is for a yellow color
- `.label-danger`: This is for a red color

Badges, on the other hand, are labels with a self collapsing nature. This means that when there's no content inside a badge, it will not appear in the HTML page. This gives you an option to create a notification icon using badges. They are mostly used for displaying numbers. Badges also do not have color variants unlike labels. Here's an example of a badge:

Bootstrap jumbotrons

Jumbotron is another useful component in Bootstrap. It's used to display large catchy headlines in a webpage. It's especially used while creating landing pages. Here's an example of a `jumbotron` class:

```
<div class="jumbotron">
  <h1>What an amazing life it is!</h1>
  <a href="#" class="btn btn-primary">Read more</a>
</div>
```

A `jumbotron` class comes with a different set of styles for heading tags and buttons. You will see the difference in font sizes of the text inside and outside the jumbotron component. The preceding code produces the following in a browser:

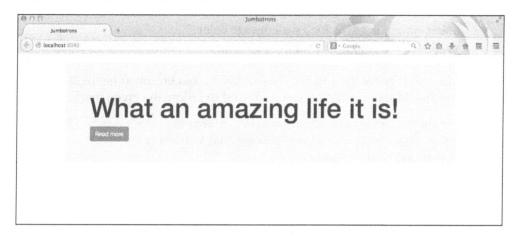

Alerts

Alerts are extremely important to communicate messages with your website users. They stand out, bright and distinguished from the rest of the page elements. You should not mistake these alerts with the alert windows in browsers. These alerts are HTML elements designed to behave like an alert.

A simple alert markup is shown in the following code:

```
<div class="alert alert-success">Message sent!</div>
```

This produces the following result in a browser:

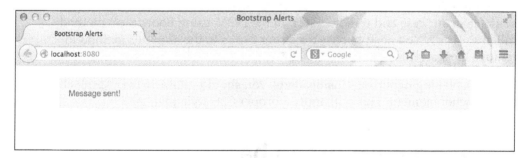

Alerts come with four different color variants:

- `.alert-success`: This varient is used for a green color
- `.alert-info`: This is used for a light blue color
- `.alert-warning`: This for a dull orange color
- `.alert-danger`: This is used for a red color

The preceding alert is not dismissible. To display a cross button at the right edge of the alert and to add the dismiss option, you need to follow the given markup:

```
<div class="alert alert-success alert-dismissible">
  <button type="button" class="close" data-dismiss="alert" >
    <span> &times; </span>
  </button>
  Message sent!
</div>
```

First, you have to add a `.alert-dismissible` class to the alert element. Next, you have to add a button element with the `.close` class. The button should also have a custom data attribute named `dismiss` with the `alert` value in it. This will let Bootstrap's JavaScript understand which component to hide when the button element is clicked on. To display a cross character inside the alert, you should add the `&times;` HTML code.

To remove an element from the DOM automatically after sometime, you can take the help of the following jQuery snippet:

```
setTimeout(function(){
  $('#alert-message').alert('close');
}, 3000);
```

In the preceding code, we used the ID of the alert message, which is `#alert-message` in our case and removed it from the DOM using Bootstrap's method called `alert()`. You need to pass the string `close` to the `alert()` method to remove the alert message.

While displaying hyperlinks inside alerts, you should give a `.alert-link` class to the anchor element. This will apply a proper CSS style to it.

Creating a progress bar

Progress bars are essential to show the progress of an action to the users. You can create attractive progress bars easily using Bootstrap's markup.

Here's the markup for a basic progress bar:

```
<div class="progress">
  <div class="progress-bar" style="width: 60%;"></div>
</div>
```

The progress bar should be wrapped inside a `div` element with the `.progress` class. This `div` element behaves as a container for the progress bar. The actual progress is shown using a child div element with the `.progress-bar` class. You can write a JavaScript code to change the CSS width of this element to see the transition of the progress bar.

The preceding progress bar looks like the following in a browser:

To add a label to the progress bar, you can add text inside the `.progress-bar` element. Take the text in the following code as an example:

```
<div class="progress">
  <div class="progress-bar" style="width: 60%;">60%</div>
</div>
```

This produces the percentage of the action's progress, as shown in the following screenshot:

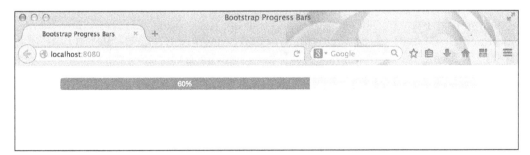

You can change the color of the .progress-bar element by adding the following classes:

- .progress-bar-success: This is for a green color
- .progress-bar-info: This is for a light blue color
- .progress-bar-danger: This is for a red color
- .progress-bar-warning: This is for a yellow color

Now comes the interesting part! You can add stripes to the progress bar by adding an additional class, .progress-bar-striped to the .progress-bar element.

```
<div class="progress">
  <div class="progress-bar progress-bar-striped" style="width:
    60%;">60%</div>
</div>
```

This produces the following result in the browser:

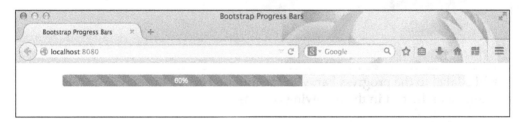

Wait! There's more. Add the .active class, along with .progress-bar-striped and see an interesting animation happening.

Panels

Bootstrap panels are box-like components that are used to place HTML components. You might want to display a box with rounded corners and a light-colored border around it. This is the component you should use in such cases.

Here's an example panel:

```
<div class="panel panel-default">
  <div class="panel-body">
    I am inside a box!
  </div>
</div>
```

This produces the following result in the browser:

The panel component becomes more interesting when you add a header and a footer to it. Yes, you read it right. Panels come with custom-designed headers and footers to create widget-like elements. If you see it carefully, you will find that the text goes inside a .panel-body element. We will now add headers and footers to the following panel:

```
<div class="panel panel-default">
  <div class="panel-heading">
    Widget 1
  </div>
  <div class="panel-body">
    I am inside a box!
  </div>
  <div class="panel-footer">
    by Syed Fazle Rahman
  </div>
</div>
```

This produces the following result in the browser:

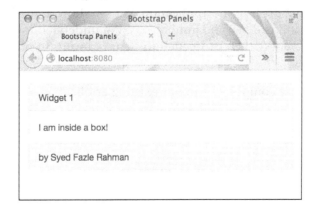

Panels also come in different colors:

- .panel-success: This is used for a green color
- .panel-primary: This is used for a dark blue color
- .panel-info: This is used for a light blue color
- .panel-warning: This is used for a yellow color
- .panel-danger : This is used for a red color

The following screenshot displays a green color panel:

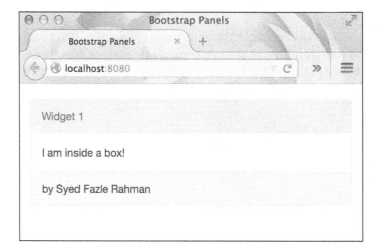

Summary

Through this chapter, we learned how to use some of the interesting and useful components of Bootstrap. These components are generally used to give a better user experience to the users of the application. We saw how to use breadcrumbs, paginations, labels and badges, and jumbotrons. We understood what alerts are and when to use them. We then proceeded to create a beautiful progress bar and widget using panels.

We will integrate these components in our existing application whenever needed in the next chapter.

8
Working with Bootstrap Modals

Every developer has used an alert/prompt window when dealing with web development. They are generally used to display important messages, accept information from the user, display warning messages, and for many different purposes. The problem with these traditional dialog windows is that they have become outdated, and our visitors probably hate them. It's no longer recommended to use dialog windows from a better user experience perspective.

To solve this problem, web developers discovered another better way to replace pop-up windows. They used a hidden HTML element inside the same web page. Whenever needed, this hidden element was displayed with the help of some JavaScript code and CSS styling. Bootstrap's modal does exactly same. It is a flexible dialog prompt with minimum required functionality. It has got its own Bootstrap styling and animation.

In this chapter, we will learn how to create a Bootstrap modal and its various types and functionalities. We will also integrate a modal component in our Rails application.

Getting started with modals

First, we will create a static application to create and test various types of Bootstrap modals. Once we are done with the basics of modals, we will proceed to integrate it in our existing `Online Shopping Rails` application.

Create a new folder called `Bootstrap Modals` in your system. Now, create a new file called `index.html` and paste the following starter template in it:

```
<!DOCTYPE html>
  <html lang="en">
```

```
<head>
  <meta charset="utf-8">
  <meta http-equiv="X-UA-Compatible" content="IE=edge">
  <meta name="viewport" content="width=device-width,
    initial-scale=1">
  <title>Bootstrap Modals</title>
  <!-- Bootstrap -->
  <link rel="stylesheet"href="http://maxcdn.bootstrapcdn.com/
    bootstrap/3.2.0/css/bootstrap.min.css">
</head>
<body>
  <h1>Hello World</h1>
  <!-- jQuery (necessary for Bootstrap's JavaScript plugins) -->
  <script src="https://ajax.googleapis.com/ajax/libs/jquery/
    1.11.1/jquery.min.js"></script>
  <!-- Include all compiled plugins (below), or include
    individual files as needed -->
  <script src="http://maxcdn.bootstrapcdn.com/bootstrap/3.2.0/
    js/bootstrap.min.js"></script>
</body>
</html>
```

Let's delete the `Hello World` tag from the preceding template and insert the markup needed for a modal. To create a modal, we need to define a `<div>` element with a `.modal` class:

```
<div class="modal">
</div>
```

Optionally, you can also add the `.fade` class to apply the `.fade-in` animation to the modal:

```
<div class="modal fade">
</div>
```

The `.modal` class creates a wrapper for the modal component. It hides the HTML web page's scrolling attribute by setting the CSS `overflow` property to `hidden`. It also creates an HTML area with `fixed` positioning on top of all the HTML elements present on the same page.

Next, we will add a markup for placing contents inside the modal. The procedure goes as follows:

```
<div class="modal fade">
  <div class="modal-dialog">
```

```
      <div class="modal-content">
      </div>
    </div>
  </div>
```

The classes `.modal-dialog` and `.modal-content` are, together, responsible for properly centering a white-colored content area in a modal component.

Let's proceed to create the modal's body area for placing the HTML contents inside a modal:

```
<div class="modal fade">
  <div class="modal-dialog">
    <div class="modal-content">
      <div class="modal-body">
        <p>The content goes here.</p>
      </div>
    </div>
  </div>
</div>
```

You can place any HTML element, as per your requirement, inside this `.modal-body` div. You can use it to display a long `Terms & Conditions` text, a `login` form, a warning text, and so on.

We are ready with our first basic modal. If you load this HTML page inside the browser, you will find a blank page. It's because we have created a modal, but didn't create any element which will trigger this modal. Modals are hidden components in Bootstrap.

Let's create a Bootstrap button to trigger the preceding modal when clicked on:

```
<button class="btn btn-primary" data-toggle="modal" data-target="#myFirstModal">
  Show Modal
</button>
```

This button should have two very important custom attributes to trigger a modal: `data-toggle` and `data-target`. The first attribute tells Bootstrap's JavaScript which component it's concerned with, while the second attribute specifies which particular modal to open. The second attribute holds the ID of the modal you want to open. Let's also apply this ID to our preceding modal. Hence, the final markup for our modal should look like the following:

```
<div class="modal fade" id="myFirstModal">
  <div class="modal-dialog">
```

```
        <div class="modal-content">
          <div class="modal-body">
            <p>The content goes here.</p>
          </div>
        </div>
      </div>
    </div>
```

You should get a modal that looks like the one shown in the following screenshot:

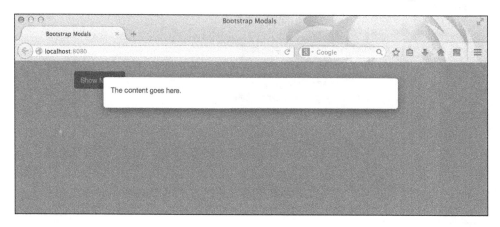

A modal component also has a header and footer area, apart from the .modal-body area. They are created using the .modal-header and .modal-footer classes. We can apply a header and footer by adding code, as follows:

```
<div class="modal fade" id="myFirstModal">
  <div class="modal-dialog">
    <div class="modal-content">
      <div class="modal-header">
        <h4 class="modal-title">This is a modal</h4>
      </div>
      <div class="modal-body">
        <p>The content goes here.</p>
      </div>
      <div class="modal-footer">
        <p>This is the footer.</p>
      </div>
    </div>
  </div>
</div>
```

It is recommended that you use an `<h4>` tag with a `.modal-title` class inside `.modal-header`. All the default elements inside the modal's footer will appear right, aligned, as per Bootstrap's CSS. You can modify it by overriding its CSS property:

```
.modal-footer{

text-align: left;
}
```

The preceding modal a with a header and footer should look like this:

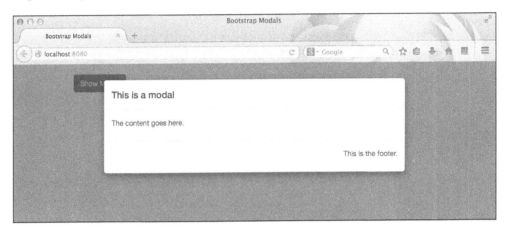

Changing Bootstrap's modal size

Bootstrap's modals also come in various sizes: large, normal, and small. You need to use the following classes to change the size of the modal:

- `.modal-lg`: This is for larger modals
- No class: This is for normal sized modals
- `.modal-sm`: This is for smaller modals

You have to add the preceding classes to the `.modal-dialog` element in the modal's markup. Take the following code as an example:

```
<div class="modal fade" id="myFirstModal">
  <div class="modal-dialog modal-lg">
    <div class="modal-content">
      <div class="modal-header">
        <h4 class="modal-title">This is a modal</h4>
      </div>
      <div class="modal-body">
```

```
      <p>The content goes here.</p>
    </div>
    <div class="modal-footer">
      <p>This is the footer.</p>
    </div>
   </div>
  </div>
</div>
```

The preceding markup will create a larger modal, as shown in the following screenshot:

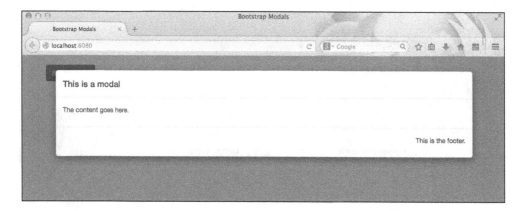

Additional Bootstrap modal features

Bootstrap provides many features for the modal component. These features are generally provided as JSON properties, while triggering the modal component. Alternatively, you can use these features by using custom data-* attributes in the .modal element. Bootstrap's additional features are:

- data-backdrop: This attribute accepts static or true values. When set to static, it disables the closing of the modal when clicked outside the modal body.

- data-keyboard: This accepts Boolean values and is set to true by default. When true, features of data-keyboard closes the modal when the *Esc* key is pressed.

- data-show: This accepts Boolean values and is set to false by default. When true, data-shows the modal when it was initialized.

Fetching remote content from a Bootstrap modal

Here, `data-remote` is a special data attribute in Bootstrap's modal component. It is used to load a remote web page inside a modal, when data is triggered. This feature is only available from Bootstrap v 3.0 to v 3.2.0; I believe it is really very useful!

Let's check out an example of how to use it.

Let's create a new HTML page named `page2.html` inside the same Bootstrap Model project folder. Place the following basic HTML inside it:

```
<!DOCTYPE html>
<html>
  <head>
    <title>Page 2</title>
  </head>
  <body>
    <div class="container">
      <h1>Hello World from Page 2</h1>
    </div>
  </body>
</html>
```

This page should look like the following in a browser:

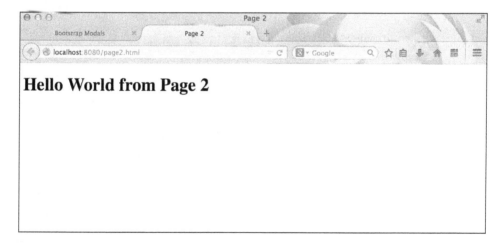

We will now load this page inside our previous modal, whenever it is triggered. Modify the previously created modal markup, as follows:

```
<div class="modal fade" id="myFirstModal" data-
   remote="page2.html">
   <div class="modal-dialog">
     <div class="modal-content">
       <div class="modal-header">
         <h4 class="modal-title">This is a modal</h4>
       </div>
       <div class="modal-body">
         <p>The content goes here.</p>
       </div>
       <div class="modal-footer">
         <p>This is the footer.</p>
       </div>
     </div>
   </div>
</div>
```

Note that this time we have added an additional attribute `data-remote`, and the path to `page2.html` as the value. Let's refresh the browser and trigger the modal. This time, you should see `page2.html` loaded inside the modal instead of the default content. The screenshot is as follows:

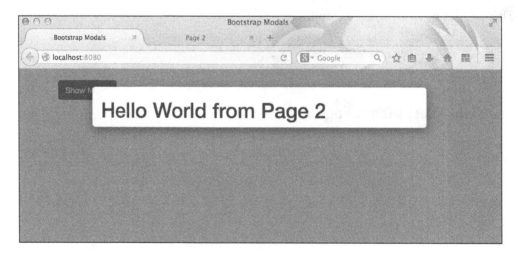

 You should be very careful while using cross-domain links as remote content. Many browsers might not allow that.

Using Bootstrap's modal in a Rails application

In our Demo Shopping Application, created in previous chapters, we had all the products listed in a single page. We will add an additional button, named **Buy,** beside the **Show** button in each product. When a user clicks on the **Buy** button, the browser will display a modal confirming his/her action to add the particular product to the cart. The modal will have an **Add to cart** button, which will simulate the behavior of the product that is being added to the cart and then will close the modal. We won't be creating a real shopping cart in this book. It's up to you to decide which method you would like to use to create a shopping cart.

Open the application.html.erb file present in the layouts folder by navigating to **app | views | layouts**. We will create a global modal in this file. This modal will get triggered whenever the **Buy** button is clicked. The markup for this modal is as follows:

```
<div class="modal fade" id="buyModal">
  <div class="modal-dialog">
    <div class="modal-content">
      <div class="modal-body">
        <p>Are you sure you want to buy this?</p>
        <button class="btn btn-success">
          <i class="glyphicon glyphicon-plus"></i> Add to cart
        </button>
      </div>
    </div>
  </div>
</div>
```

Make sure that you place this modal markup outside the entire markup that was previously created. Bootstrap recommends you to always place a modal's markup in the topmost level.

Now, we are done with placing a dummy modal. Let's proceed to create a **Buy** button.

Open the index.html.erb file present inside the products folder by navigating to **app | views | products**. Search for the previously created **Show** button, which had the following code:

```
<%= link_to 'Show', product, :class=>"btn btn-primary" %>
```

We will place another button with no `href` attribute and add custom data attributes to trigger the modal:

```
<%= link_to 'Buy', '#', :class=>"btn btn-success" %>
```

This will create a new **Buy** button beside each **Show** button.

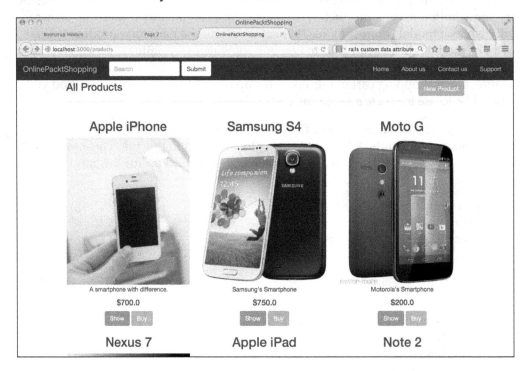

Let's add custom data attributes to trigger the modal component. Modify the **Buy** button, as follows:

```
<%= link_to 'Buy', '#', :class=>"btn btn-success", :data=> { :toggle
=>'modal', :target=>'#buyModal' } %>
```

Here, the `data-target` attribute will hold the `#buyModal` value, which is also the ID of our modal.

Now, if you click on the **Buy** button, it will display the modal, as shown in the following screenshot:

Let's add a functionality which will dismiss the modal when we click on the Add to cart button. For this, we need to again edit the application.html.erb file. We have to add an extra data attribute data-dismiss with the value as modal to the **Add to cart** button. Let's add the data attribute:

```
<button class="btn btn-success" data-dismiss="modal"><i
class="glyphicon glyphicon-plus"></i> Add to cart</button>
```

Adding the preceding data attribute will let Bootstrap's JavaScript know which component to close.

Summary

I hope you enjoyed learning how to create a flexible Bootstrap modal component. Through this chapter, we learnt how to create a basic modal in a static project. We then moved on to add extra functionalities to it. We also saw how to create modals of different sizes by using additional classes such as `.modal-lg` and `.modal-sm`. Finally, we integrated a modal component to our shopping application. We learnt how to simulate the `Add to cart` functionality through the dummy confirm modal. The field is now open for you to experiment more with modals.

In the next chapter, we are going to understand one of the most interesting Bootstrap components, Carousels. We will see how we can use the carousel component and create beautiful image slideshows.

9
Creating Image Slideshows with Bootstrap Carousel

The term **Carousel** is inspired from the real-world carousel, which is found in many recreational parks. It rotates the circular structure on which people stand/sit, repeatedly, A web-based carousel behaves similarly. It is a slideshow of images and their respective textual data.

Carousels are one of the most important web components. They are extremely useful for shopping websites to display many products fashionably. Many blogging websites also take advantage of this component.

If you are a novice web designer, then creating a carousel for your own website can be a little complicated. Bootstrap 3, on the other hand, provides a great JavaScript plugin called carousel, which is ready to use.

You have to write many lines of JavaScript and CSS code to create a beautiful image slideshow using Bootstrap. Just like the previous components of Bootstrap, you have to put the right markup in place.

We will cover the following topics in this chapter:

- Getting started with Bootstrap Carousel
- Adding captions to the slides
- Customizing the carousel

Getting started with Bootstrap Carousel

Let's get started with Bootstrap Carousel component and create a basic image slideshow. As always, we will be creating a static HTML page for this, to learn how it is used. The steps are as follows:

1. Create a new folder called `Bootstrap Carousel` anywhere you like in your system. We will use the same static markup for the `index.html` file:

```
<!DOCTYPE html>
<html lang="en">
  <head>
    <meta charset="utf-8">
    <meta http-equiv="X-UA-Compatible" content="IE=edge">
    <meta name="viewport" content="width=device-width,
      initial-scale=1">
    <title>Bootstrap Carousel</title>
    <!-- Bootstrap -->
    <link rel="stylesheet" href="http://maxcdn.bootstrapcdn.com/
      bootstrap/3.2.0/css/bootstrap.min.css">
  </head>
  <body>
    <h1>Hello World</h1>
    <!-- jQuery (necessary for Bootstrap's JavaScript plugins) -->
    <script src="https://ajax.googleapis.com/ajax/libs/jquery/
      1.11.1/jquery.min.js"></script>
    <!-- Include all compiled plugins (below), or include
      individual files as needed -->
    <script src="http://maxcdn.bootstrapcdn.com/bootstrap/3.2.0/
      js/bootstrap.min.js"></script>
  </body>
</html>
```

2. Let's remove the `Hello World` markup from the preceding file and start building our first carousel component.

3. Bootstrap Carousel is divided into three major parts: indicator, inner wrapper, and controls. Each one of them has their own importance. To create a Bootstrap Carousel, we need to create a `div` element with the class `.carousel`:

```
<div class="carousel">
</div>
```

4. Bootstrap allows you to create a slideshow, with and without sliding animation. If you want the slide items to have a nice sliding effect, add a class `.slide` with the `.carousel` class:

```
<div class="carousel slide">
</div>
```

5. There's an optional `data-ride` attribute that you can add to the preceding `div` element. It is used to mark a carousel as animating, starting at page load. Let's set this attribute as well:

```
<div class="carousel slide" data-ride="carousel">
</div>
```

6. We will also add an ID attribute to this `div` element. This attribute will be used various times while defining the child elements of the carousel:

```
<div class="carousel slide" data-ride="carousel" id="my-first-
carousel">
</div>
```

7. We will now proceed to create `Inner-Wrapper` of the carousel component. This wrapper will hold all the sliding items of the carousel:

```
<div class="carousel slide" data-ride="carousel"
  id="my-first-carousel">
  <div class="carousel-inner">
  </div>
</div>
```

8. We will start inserting the sliding elements into this `Inner-Wrapper`. Each sliding item should have a `.item` class attached to it:

```
<div class="carousel slide" data-ride="carousel"
  id="my-first-carousel">
  <div class="carousel-inner">
    <div class="item">
    </div>
  </div>
</div>
```

9. There's no limit to the number of items you can add to a carousel component. Let's proceed and fill this item with an image to represent the item:

```
<div class="carousel slide" data-ride="carousel"
  id="my-first-carousel">
  <div class="carousel-inner">
    <div class="item">
      <img src="link/to/image1.jpg" alt="Slide 1">
    </div>
    <div class="item">
      <img src="link/to/image2.jpg" alt="Slide 2">
    </div>
    <div class="item">
      <img src="link/to/image3.jpg" alt="Slide 3">
    </div>
    <div class="item">
      <img src="link/to/image4.jpg" alt="Slide 4">
    </div>
  </div>
</div>
```

10. Now, we have four sliding items, each filled with a unique image. It's time to tell Bootstrap which item should be represented as the first item of the slideshow.

11. This can be done by adding a class .active to any one .item element. In our case, we will add the .active class to the first .item element:

```
<div class="carousel slide" data-ride="carousel"
  id="my-first-carousel">
  <div class="carousel-inner">
    <div class="item active">
      <img src="link/to/image1.jpg" alt="Slide 1">
    </div>
    <div class="item">
      <img src="link/to/image2.jpg" alt="Slide 2">
    </div>
  </div>
</div>
```

12. We are now done with a basic carousel that has four sliding items in it.
    Let's view it in the browser:

13. We have two important elements missing from this slideshow: indicators
    and controls. Indicators are very useful to directly jump on a particular slide.
    Controls let us navigate through the slides one by one in either direction.

Let's proceed and add them too. Indicators are created using an ordered list with the `.carousel-indicators` class:

```
<div class="carousel slide" data-ride="carousel"
  id="my-first-carousel">
  <!-- Indicators →
  <ol class="carousel-indicators">
  </ol>
  <div class="carousel-inner">
  </div>
</div>
```

Each `<li>` item in the indicator is a handle for a particular slide in the carousel. They should have two different data attributes: `data-target` and `data-slide-to`. The `data-target` attribute is used to indicate which carousel we are talking about in a web page. It should hold the ID of the carousel element that is, `#my-first-carousel`. `data-slide-to` is used to indicate the slide number on which the content/image is presented. For example, if you have four slides, the slide numbers are from 0 to 3:

```
<div class="carousel slide" data-ride="carousel"
  id="my-first-carousel">
  <!-- Indicators →
  <ol class="carousel-indicators">
    <li data-target="#my-first-carousel"
      data-slide-to="0" class="active"></li>
    <li data-target="#my-first-carousel"
      data-slide-to="1"></li>
    <li data-target="#my-first-carousel" data-slide-
      to="2"></li>
    <li data-target="#my-first-carousel" data-slide-
      to="3"></li>
  </ol>
  <div class="carousel-inner">
  </div>
</div>
```

14. If you check the page in the browser, you can see that the indicators appear at the bottom of the carousel:

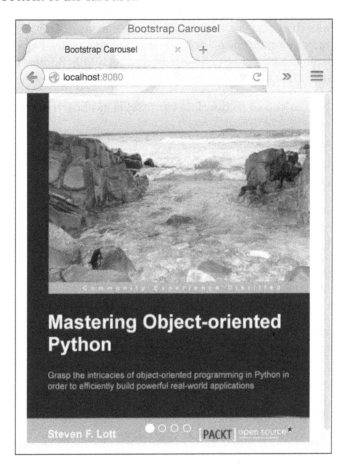

Let's add `controls` to the carousel. Controls are a pair of HTML anchor elements `<a>` with a set of attributes, as shown:

```
<a class="left carousel-control"
  href="#my-first-carousel" data-slide="prev">
  <span class="glyphicon glyphicon-chevron-left"></span>
</a>
<a class="right carousel-control" href=
  "#my-first-carousel"   data-slide="next">
  <span class="glyphicon glyphicon-chevron-right"></span>
</a>
```

Each anchor element has a class `.carousel-control`. Additionally, you have to add directional classes `.left` and `.right` to each one of `.carousel-control` element, respectively. These directional classes help them to take their respective position in the carousel. The `href` property of each anchor element must point to the parent carousel element using ID. We also have a `data-slide` attribute which tells Bootstrap which slide to navigate to from the current slide.

15. Finally, the markup of a complete carousel is as shown in the following code:

```html
<div id="my-first-carousel" class="carousel slide"
  data-ride="carousel">
<!-- Indicators -->
  <ol class="carousel-indicators">
    <li data-target="#my-first-carousel"
      data-slide-to="0" class="active"></li>
    <li data-target="#my-first-carousel"
      data-slide-to="1"></li>
    <li data-target="#my-first-carousel"
      data-slide-to="2"></li>
    <li data-target="#my-first-carousel"
      data-slide-to="3"></li>
  </ol>
  <!-- Wrapper for slides -->
  <div class="carousel-inner">
    <div class="item active">
      <img src="images/book1.jpg" alt="Book 1">
    </div>
    <div class="item">
      <img src="images/book2.jpg" alt="Book 2">
    </div>
    <div class="item">
      <img src="images/book3.jpg" alt="Book 3">
    </div>
    <div class="item">
      <img src="images/book4.jpg" alt="Book 4">
    </div>
  </div>
  <!-- Controls -->
  <a class="left carousel-control"
    href="#my-first-carousel" data-slide="prev">
    <span class="glyphicon glyphicon-chevron-left"></span>
```

```
  </a>
  <a class="right carousel-control" href="#my-first-
    carousel" data-slide="next">
  <span class="glyphicon glyphicon-chevron-right"></span>
  </a>
</div>
```

You can also see the controls appearing on the carousel in the following screenshot. To control the slideshow using a keyboard, you need to add the `data-keyboard` attribute with the value as `true` to the `.carousel` element:

Adding captions to the slides

Captions can be easily added to each slide item by inserting a `div` element with the `.carousel-caption` class. This element will hold two different elements: a `heading` and `paragraph` element. You have the liberty to use either one of them or both. Take the following code as an example:

```
<div class="item">
  <img src="images/book1.jpg" alt="Book 1">
    <div class="carousel-caption">
    <h3>This is the first slideshow</h3>
    <p>Lorem ipsum donor.</p>
  </div>
</div>
```

Customizing Carousel

You can also add various, different `data-*` attributes to `.carousel` to change its default behavior. Bootstrap provides three different attributes:

`data-interval`: This attribute is used to change the duration time for each slide. It accepts integer values in milliseconds. For example, `data-interval="5000"`.

`data-pause`: This attribute takes only one value, `hover`. When this attribute is set, the slideshow pauses when the mouse is hovered over it.

`data-wrap`: This attribute accepts Boolean values. When set as `true`, the slideshow will begin again from the first slide automatically.

Summary

In this chapter, we saw how to create a basic carousel. We added various elements such as indicators, controls, and captions to it. We also saw various customization options available in Bootstrap.

In the next chapter, we will implement all that we have learned in Bootstrap.

10
Creating a Shopping Cart Using Bootstrap Modals

This chapter is all about implementing what we have learned so far in Bootstrap. We won't be learning anything new here, but this chapter will definitely clear some of the core concepts such as using Bootstrap modal, typography, buttons, and responsive tables.

In this chapter, we will create a JavaScript modal that will serve as a shopping cart in our Shopping application. This cart will have all the features needed for any shopping website. For demo purposes, we will be displaying only static data in our shopping cart.

In a nutshell, we will cover the following topics:

- Adding a shopping cart symbol
- Creating a shopping cart using modals

Adding a shopping cart symbol

Before proceeding to create a shopping cart in our application, we need a handle which when clicked on, will display the shopping cart. For our application, I will add a Glyphicon font icon to display an icon in the current navigation bar of our application. So, let's proceed and make this tweak.

Navigate to **app** | **views** | **layouts** and edit the `application.html.erb` file. Just in front case of the `<li>` element of **Home** , add another `<li>` element with the Glyphicon icon of the shopping cart, as follows:

```
<li><a href="#"><span class="glyphicon glyphicon-shopping-
    cart"></span></a></li>
```

 Remember, Glyphicons are font images provided by Bootstrap, by default, in its repository.

Open the browser and check for the shopping cart symbol in the navigation bar. It should look like the one shown in the following screenshot:

We will add a number beside the shopping cart icon to indicate the number of products added to the shopping cart. We will use Bootstrap's badges for this. Adding a `<span>` element with the class `.badge` will create a beautiful number indicator:

```
<li><a href="#"><span class="glyphicon glyphicon-shopping-
    cart"></span> <span class="badge">4</span></a></li>
```

You should have a number indicator in the navigation bar, as shown in the following screenshot:

Let's also add the custom data attributes needed to trigger a modal in this shopping cart link. As stated in the earlier chapter, we need two custom attributes to create a modal handle: `data-target` and `data-toggle`. So, let's add these attributes to our shopping cart link:

```
<li><a href="#" data-target="#shoppingCart" data-
    toggle="modal"><span class="glyphicon glyphicon-shopping-
        cart"></span> <span class="badge">4</span></a></li>
```

Here, the value provided to data-target is `#shoppingCart`. Hence, we will use `shoppingCart` as the ID of the modal that we will create in the next section.

Now, we are ready with a shopping cart icon that will trigger our shopping cart modal when clicked. This icon also represents the number of items present inside the shopping cart. Impressive! Isn't it?

Creating a shopping cart using modals

As stated earlier in this book, to create a Bootstrap modal, we need a `<div>` element with the `.modal` class. We will also add the `.fade` class to apply the fading transition. It is the only transition animation provided by Bootstrap.

1. At end of the `application.html.erb` file, add the markup for the modal, as follows:

   ```
   <div class="modal fade">
   </div>
   ```

2. One of the most important things to note here, is that we have two modals in this page. To uniquely identify each one of them, we should give different IDs to them. In this case, we already have an ID with us, which is `shoppingCart`. So, let's add it to our markup:

   ```
   <div class="modal fade" id="shoppingCart">
   </div>
   ```

3. Next, we need to place a markup for a modal dialog and modal content:

   ```
   <div class="modal fade" id="shoppingCart">
     <div class="modal-dialog modal-lg">
       <div class="modal-content">
       </div>
     </div>
   </div>
   ```

   Compared to the modal created in the earlier chapter, we are using a larger modal here, with the help of the `.modal-lg` class.

4. Now, we will add a header to our modal. This header will contain the title **Your Cart** with another text that will indicate the number of items present in the shopping cart:

```
<div class="modal-header">
<p class="pull-right text-primary"><b>4 items</b></p>
<h4 class="modal-title text-primary"><span class="glyphicon
glyphicon-shopping-cart"></span> Your Cart </h4>
</div>
```

5. Place the preceding content inside the `.modal-content` element. The `<p>` element is floated towards the right using the class `.pull-right` and colored dark blue using the `.text-primary` utility class. It is used to represent the number of items present inside the shopping cart. The title **Your Cart** is written using the `<h4>` element with the `.modal-title` and `.text-primary` class (to add a blue color to the text). We also have an icon of a shopping cart present inside the title, created using the Glyphicon icon. If you trigger this modal by clicking on the shopping cart icon you will see something like the following:

Let's proceed to create the body part of the modal. Perform the following steps to create the body of the modal:

1. Add .modal-header;. to the following markup, as the sibling of the

```
<div class="modal-body">
</div>
```

2. We will insert a Bootstrap table that will hold the actual item details:

```
<div class="modal-body">:
   <table class="table table-bordered">
   </table>
</div>
```

3. Let's create multiple columns inside this table:

```
<div class="modal-body">
   <table class="table table-bordered">
     <tr>
       <th>Sl no</th>
```

```
        <th>Item Name</th>
        <th>Unit Price (USD)</th>
        <th>Quantity</th>
        <th>Price</th>
        <th></th>
      </tr>
    </table>
</div>
```

We have columns for **Serial no**, **Item Name**, **Unit Price**, **Quantity Ordered**, and **Price of the item**. We also have an extra column without a heading that will contain a link to remove a particular item row from the table.

4. Let's fill up the first row:

```
<div class="modal-body">
  <table class="table table-bordered">
    <tr>
      <th>Sl no</th>
      <th>Item Name</th>
      <th>Unit Price (USD)</th>
      <th>Quantity</th>
      <th>Price</th>
      <th></th>
    </tr>
    <tr>
      <td>1</td>
      <td>Apple iPhone 6</td>
      <td>$399</td>
      <td>
      <input type="text" class="form-control" value="1"
        placeholder="Enter Quantity" style="width:
          50px;" />
      </td>
      <td>$399</td>
      <td><a href="#" class="btn btn-danger btn-
        sm">remove</a></td>
    </tr>
  </table>
</div>
```

5. For the quantity field, I have used an input field with the `.form-control` class to give a Bootstrap look and feel to it. I have also applied a CSS width of `50px` to it. In the last column, I have added a text link called **remove** with the `.btn`, `.btn-danger`, and `.btn-sm` class. The `.btn-danger` class makes the button red, while the `.btn-sm` class is used to reduce the size of the normal Bootstrap button. Try filling up some more items in the table. Finally, you will get a modal that looks like the one shown in the following screenshot:

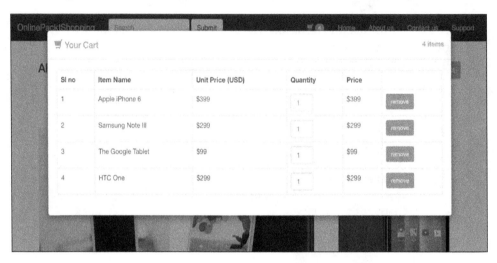

6. We are now left with the last row that will display the total sum of the items. Let's proceed and add that too:

```
<tr class="active lead">
  <td colspan="4">Total</td>
    <td>$1,096</td>
    <td><a href="#" class="btn btn-danger btn-sm">
      clear all</a>
  </td>
</tr>
```

Instead of adding all the columns, I have merged the first four columns by using the `colspan` attribute here. In the last column, I have changed the text of the button to **clear all**. One of the most important changes here are the classes .active and .lead added to the row. The .active class highlights the row using a grey-colored background, whereas the .lead class increases the font size of the text. The modal should now look like the following:

7. We will now add two different buttons at the end of the modal: **Continue Shopping** and **Checkout**:

```
<a href="#" class="btn btn-success pull-right">Checkout
  <span class="glyphicon glyphicon-chevron-right">
  </span>
</a>
<a href="#" class="btn btn-default" data-dismiss="modal">
  Continue Shopping
</a>
```

The first button is pulled towards the right using the `.pull-right` utility class. The **Continue Shopping** button uses the `data-dismiss` attribute to close the modal and to let the user continue using the website.

8. Finally, our Shopping cart design is complete. It should now look like the one shown in the following screenshot:

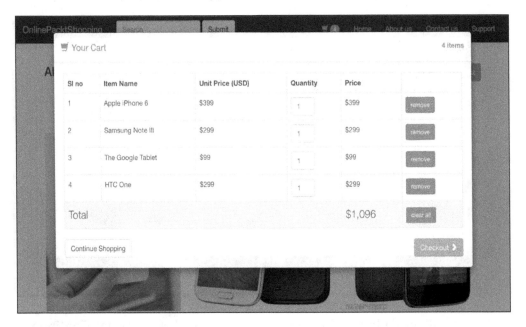

Summary

I hope you enjoyed reading this chapter. Through this chapter, we tried to design a dummy shopping cart using Bootstrap and its components. We saw how to use Bootstrap tables inside Bootstrap modals, and how to make use of Bootstrap's utility classes. We have also seen how to use free font icons, Glyphicons, to create shopping cart icons inside a navigation bar.

In the next chapter, we are going to learn one of the most important topics, *Customizing Bootstrap*. Be prepared and join me soon.

Adding Custom Styles to a Rails Application

Finally, we have reached the last chapter of this book, where we will talk about how to add a custom styles to a Rails application, which is powered by Bootstrap framework. Throughout the book, we have gone through various Bootstrap CSS and JavaScript components that come ready to use out of the box.

In this chapter, we will see how to extend Bootstrap framework and add our own style to it. There are still many important components that are missing from the Bootstrap framework. We will check out some of the popular Bootstrap plugins that are available for free.

The topics that we will cover are:

- Adding Bootstrap-sass to a Rails Application
- Customizing Bootstrap through variables

Adding Bootstrap-sass to a Rails application

In the *Installing Bootstrap in the Rails project*, section in *chapter 2, Introducing Bootstrap 3* we saw how to include Bootstrap into our Rails application through three different ways:

- The CDN method
- Bootstrap-sass gem
- By downloading Bootstrap files

To quicken things up, we had opted for the CDN method. Well, in this chapter, we are going to use Bootstrap through Bootstrap-sass gem. This will enable us to completely customize the Bootstrap's default styles. So, let's proceed and install `Bootstrap-sass` gem in our application:

1. Go to the `application` folder and edit the file `Gemfile` using a text editor. Add the following two lines of code at the end of this file:

```
gem 'bootstrap-sass', '~> 3.3.1'
gem 'autoprefixer-rails'
```

2. The above two lines will install `bootstrap-sass` and `autoprefixer-rails` gems into your application. The `autoprefixer-rails` is needed to automatically append browser vendor prefixes in the CSS `stylesheets`.

3. Let's bundle the application, so that the above gems are actually downloaded and installed in our application.

```
bundle install
```

4. Once the execution of the above command is complete, navigate to the `app | assets | stylesheets` folder. Rename the `application.css` file to the `application.css.scss` file. Next, remove the imported CDN link from the file, which was included by us earlier.

5. Now, we need to include Bootstrap files that are downloaded through gem inside the `application.css.scss` file. To do that, include the following 2 lines:

```
@import "bootstrap-sprockets";
@import "bootstrap";
```

The `bootstrap-sprockets` value is needed to correctly link the font files with the Bootstrap's CSS files.

It's time to link the Bootstrap's JavaScript files using the recently gem:

1. First, we need to remove the hardcoded Bootstrap's JavaScript CDN link from the `application.html.erb` file, present in the `layouts` folder by navigating to `app | views | layouts` folder. Remove the following line from this file:

```
<script
  src="//netdna.bootstrapcdn.com/bootstrap/3.2.0/js
    /bootstrap.min.js">
</script>
```

2. Next, go to the JavaScript folder by navigating to `app | assets | javascript` folder and edit the `application.js` file. Add the following line immediately after the jQuery line:

```
//= require bootstrap-sprockets
```

3. Finally, we are done. If you reopen your application in the browser, you can see that everything is working, just like before.

Customizing Bootstrap through variables

Most of the visible Bootstrap styles can be overridden simply by using pre-defined Bootstrap variables. Before proceeding, you should understand that Bootstrap was initially compatible with LESS only. They have later ported it to the Sass version.

LESS and Sass are CSS preprocessors that help us to organize and write scalable CSS styles. Both of them are very similar to each other in syntax and differ only by the additional features that one has and the other doesn't.

Hence, all the variables present in the LESS version remain the same in the Sass version, as well. Bootstrap hasn't provided a dedicated page for the list of variables present in Sass, however, you can find the list of variables in the LESS version on their official website (`http://getbootstrap.com/customize/#less-variables`). Let's proceed and change some of the default Bootstrap styles.

In our application, we have used `btn-success` at various places. So, let's change some of the CSS styles in it. Re-open the `application.css.scss` file, and add the following lines before the Bootstrap's import line:

```
$btn-success-color: #333;
$btn-success-bg: #AEDBAE;
$btn-success-border: darken($btn-success-bg, 5%);
```

We can change the style of the `.btn-success` class completely through the `$btn-success-color`, `$btn-success-bg`, and `$btn-success-border` Bootstrap Sass variables. In the above code, I have changed the text color of the button to #333. I have also lightened the background color to a new HEX color, and finally changed the border color using the darken color function in Sass.

You can go through the whole list of available variables and make the customizations accordingly. You can also include the available Bootstrap theme by adding the following line in the `application.css.scss` file:

```
@import "bootstrap/theme";
```

The `bootstrap/theme` is the official Bootstrap's default style customized from Bootstrap's theme. It comes with some cool styles and you should try using it.

Summary

Bootstrap customization can help you create a visually different looking website. If you are a designer in the Rails application development team, this is the field you must master. In this chapter, we saw how to include Bootstrap-sass gem in a Rails application. We also understood what it takes to override the default Bootstrap styles through pre-defined variables. I hope you found this useful.

In the end, if you still have questions related to using Bootstrap in Rails applications shoot me a tweet `@fazlerocks`, I will be happy to help you!

Index

Thank you for buying
Bootstrap for Rails

About Packt Publishing

Packt, pronounced 'packed', published its first book, *Mastering phpMyAdmin for Effective MySQL Management*, in April 2004, and subsequently continued to specialize in publishing highly focused books on specific technologies and solutions.

Our books and publications share the experiences of your fellow IT professionals in adapting and customizing today's systems, applications, and frameworks. Our solution-based books give you the knowledge and power to customize the software and technologies you're using to get the job done. Packt books are more specific and less general than the IT books you have seen in the past. Our unique business model allows us to bring you more focused information, giving you more of what you need to know, and less of what you don't.

Packt is a modern yet unique publishing company that focuses on producing quality, cutting-edge books for communities of developers, administrators, and newbies alike. For more information, please visit our website at www.packtpub.com.

About Packt Open Source

In 2010, Packt launched two new brands, Packt Open Source and Packt Enterprise, in order to continue its focus on specialization. This book is part of the Packt Open Source brand, home to books published on software built around open source licenses, and offering information to anybody from advanced developers to budding web designers. The Open Source brand also runs Packt's Open Source Royalty Scheme, by which Packt gives a royalty to each open source project about whose software a book is sold.

Writing for Packt

We welcome all inquiries from people who are interested in authoring. Book proposals should be sent to author@packtpub.com. If your book idea is still at an early stage and you would like to discuss it first before writing a formal book proposal, then please contact us; one of our commissioning editors will get in touch with you.

We're not just looking for published authors; if you have strong technical skills but no writing experience, our experienced editors can help you develop a writing career, or simply get some additional reward for your expertise.

Building a Responsive Website with Bootstrap [Video]

ISBN: 978-1-78216-498-2   Duration: 01:56 hrs

Build unique and responsive business layouts using modern techniques with Twitter Bootstrap

1. Implement incredible Bootstrap-only features such as the grid, image carousel, and more.

2. Use Retina-ready icon fonts to make your site look awesome.

3. Learn time-saving tips and tricks to optimize your site's performance.

Bootstrap Site Blueprints

ISBN: 978-1-78216-452-4   Paperback: 304 pages

Design mobile-first responsive websites with Bootstrap 3

1. Learn the inner workings of Bootstrap 3 and create web applications with ease.

2. Quickly customize your designs working directly with Bootstrap's LESS files.

3. Leverage Bootstrap's excellent JavaScript plugins.

Please check **www.PacktPub.com** for information on our titles

open source
community experience distilled

Learning Bootstrap

ISBN: 978-1-78216-184-4   Paperback: 204 pages

Unearth the potential of Bootstrap to create responsive web pages using modern techniques

1. Understand the various facets of Bootstrap 3.x such as Base CSS and Components in a pragmatic way.

2. Leverage the power of Bootstrap with a mobile-first approach resulting in responsive web design.

3. Optimize and customize your workflow with LESS and jQuery plug-ins.

Rapid Bootstrap [Video]

ISBN: 978-1-78398-996-6   Duration: 00:35 hrs

Website development made fast and easy with Bootstrap

1. Build websites which work on any device and have a responsive layout and design.

2. Harness the power of CSS preprocessing using LESS.

3. Use time saving tips and tricks to build your websites faster.

Please check **www.PacktPub.com** for information on our titles

www.ingramcontent.com/pod-product-compliance
Lightning Source LLC
Chambersburg PA
CBHW060140060326
40690CB00018B/3924

* 9 7 8 1 7 8 3 9 8 7 2 6 9 *